Developing New Technologies for Young Children

Developing New Technologies for Young Children

edited by John Siraj-Blatchford

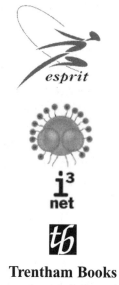

Trentham Books

Stoke on Trent, UK and Sterling, UK

Trentham Books Limited

Westview House   22883 Quicksilver Drive
734 London Road   Sterling
Oakhill   VA 20166-2012
Stoke on Trent   USA
Staffordshire
England ST4 5NP

First published 2004

British Library Cataloguing-in-Publication Data

A catalogue record for this book is available from the British Library

1 85856 307 0

Designed and typeset by Trentham Print Design Ltd., Chester and printed in Great Britain by Aldren Group Ltd., Oxford.

Contents

Preface

The work discussed in this book was carried out within the European Commission *Intelligent Information Interfaces* (i³)[1] *Experimental School Environments* (ESE) initiative which sought new proposals for research into IT-based tools or environments for 4 to 8 year olds. It was intended that successful proposals should:

> ...investigate 'new paradigms' for learning based on the development of novel IT-based tools or environments. The new paradigms investigated should make learning an enjoyable, stimulating and engaging activity, both on a personal and group level, promoting the development of key skills such as creativity, self-expression and learning to learn. (European Commission, 1997, p1)

The potential for learning was considered especially high as children were thought to be 'especially curious and open to new ideas experiences' at this age and to have 'few pre-conceptions of the world'. Ten collaborative research and development projects were subsequently funded to develop the new educational tools, along with two supporting 'working groups'. In total, a budget of more than 11 million euros was provided by the European Commission.

Although a comprehensive account of the overall achievements and findings of this major research and development initiative would be impossible in a single text, this book should contribute significantly to future technological developments for young children through its dissemination of the research findings and by pointing the way forward.

The contributions have been selected to ensure an integrated and balanced publication that will be of interest to both specialists and to more general readers concerned with the development of new technologies in early childhood. Each project is described followed by the lessons learnt in the process of developing each distinctive product. A wide range of issues concerned with the cognitive and affective development of young children have also been identified as relevant to the development of appropriate technology. Aspects of communication and collaboration, creativity and problem solving, metacognition, and of provisions for special educational needs are explored.

A distinctive characteristic of the research and developments reported here is their multi-disciplinary nature. The book thus provides a valuable and unique resource for all involved in researching the use of existing early childhood technology, as well as those embarking upon the development of new products.

The Projects

Caress created new technological and educational tools that motivated and empowered children to develop creativity, imagination and expression in interactive acoustic environments.

Construction kits made of Atoms and Bits (CAB) adapted technologies developed for older children to enable children under eight to design and construct their own cybernetic objects.

Children in Chros and Chronos (C3) was concerned with developing children's spacio-temporal reasoning through technologically enhanced and facilitated play that utilised the GPS global satellite positioning system.

éTUI developed multi-sensory programmable robotic toys that encourage children to learn about learning.

KidStory supporting collaborative story telling using virtual, zoomable interfaces and reactive spaces.

The *Networked Interactive Media in Schools (NIMIS)* project applied a range of novel ICT applications, networked computers, intuitive user interfaces and large interactive displays to develop technologically integrated and co-operative 'classrooms of the future'.

In the *Playground* project, children were empowered to design and programme their own rules into microworld games.

In *Pogo*, intuitive tools and toys were developed that would allow the children's favorite characters to move from the 'real world' into a virtual on-screen story environment.

The *Puppet* project explored new forms of early learning where the children were presented with opportunities to invent and direct stories in an innovative virtual puppet theatre.

Today's Stories sought to provide children with wearable 'KidsCam' technology that enabled them to create audio-visual diaries that simultaneously encouraged them to reflect upon their own actions, and learn from other children's perspectives in their 'reflective experiments in living'.

The Working Groups

The *Children's Awareness of Technology (CHAT)* group brought together researchers from early childhood education and developmental psychology to collaboratively develop improved understandings of children's learning associated with the wide range of information and communications technologies (ICTs) applied within the programme.

KidsLab provided a working group that supported the projects practical and informed advice on their work with young children. A central aim of the KidsLab group has involved the ongoing development and study of approaches to child-centered design of learning environments.

The importance of research and development in this area

As a number of authorities (e.g. Honey *et al*, 1999, Shakeshaft, 1999, Bosco, 2003) have been arguing for some years, it is time that researchers in the field of educational technology went beyond asking such general questions as 'Does ICT improve student outcomes', or 'Is educational ICT cost effective?' We should 'resist the technological imperative' (Selwyn, N, 1999) of researching the overall effectiveness of technology in education to focus more closely on evaluating the effects and outcomes of specific applications in the particular educational contexts of homes and classrooms. For Selwyn and many others, the primary concern should be with asking questions about:

> What is ICT being used for, by who, under which circumstances? How are learners' uses of ICT being mediated by outside-school factors (such as home/community environment, extended family and peer networks, other screen and print media) and within-school factors (such as organisational and curricular constraints, teachers, other students)? What forms are different learners' engagement with ICT taking? How is use of ICT influencing, or being influenced by, other forms of learning and how distinguishable are the 'effects' of ICT from the myriad social, cultural factors and processes in the classroom? (p1)

As Honey *et al* (1999) argue, much of the ICT research of the past has also been concerned exclusively with the effectiveness of ICT in achieving traditional learning objectives. There is little consideration of what new challenges might be undertaken if we apply technology to support children's capacities to think more critically and creatively. It is in this light that the ESE aims of developing technologies to support children's learning in terms of *creativity, self-expression and learning to learn* should be considered.

Another limitation in the dominant forms of publicly sponsored research has been that they have overwhelmingly looked back at earlier applications rather than looking forward to new ones. This too is a particular strength of the collaborative research and development established in the ESE projects. Technology moves forward quickly so that our research emphasis should be directed at least as much to the possible future applications as on present and past applications.

In 2002 the US Department of Commerce commissioned a range of experts to envisage the effects that technology might have upon education in the future. Hinrichs (2002) directly addressed the possibilities for young children. He argued that by 2020 we would see even the youngest children playing with toys that used embedded technology to capture their learning experiences by recording information about their habits and preferences. Parents would then be able to make informed choices about acquiring additional toys that would enhance their child's learning, motivation and experience. Hinrichs suggested that by 2020 preschoolers will be routinely engaging in individually chosen virtual learning environments that facilitate communication and collaboration and build upon their learning. These interactive learning environments would provide motivating contexts for collaboration and also with other children, teachers, parents, and other members of the family who would be able to play along, and also mentor them on-line. Teachers would create related classroom activities that encouraged the children to expand their abilities through real problem solving activities. Wearable technologies would be applied to facilitate the exchange, collection, communication and presentation of relevant information posted to large screen displays or holographic 3D environments. Technology would thus be applied to provide safe learning environments and video records of the children as they engage in learning activities, to support self, teacher and parent review. The children would develop long-term digital portfolios that would provide records of their achievement and allow them to share their work with others. Hinrichs' provides an enlightening 'Kindergarten 2020 Scenario':

> Alicia wakes up this morning excited about what the day will bring. Today, she gets to meet with her discovery group. This group of students has been pre-selected through learning traits collected by toys that she used prior to entering kindergarten and shared with the school upon enrollment. The group has similar interests and meets 3 days a week. Today, they are going on a virtual safari to Africa.

> Alicia likes animals a great deal and the group is going to experience how elephant families are similar to her own. Upon entering the virtual safari, she immediately experiences the size and weight of the elephants as they are presented in a 3-D environment where she feels as if she could reach out and touch them. During the safari, the virtual mentor points out how elephants are similar to our families and how important the mother is to the survival of the babies. Alicia gets to name one of the baby elephants and she and her teacher send a message to her mom telling her of Alicia's new friend.

> During the day, Alicia demonstrated two acts of kindness towards another student. She received a personalised award at the end of the day. A copy of the award was immediately forwarded to her parents. Her dad, while travelling, received notice on his cell phone that Alicia was recognised in school and calls up a video interface to share his excitement with her. When Alicia arrives home she finds balloons waiting complete with her mother's outstretched arms. (op cit, p.2-3)

In terms of technology it is already clear that all these ideas are achievable, although many readers will be surprised at how many have already been realised in the ESE projects. But as Bill Gates wrote in his introduction to Hinrichs' paper, we do still have quite a long way to go before we can see how much technology can really do to support learning:

> Solving business problems with computers looks easy when compared to the often complex and little-understood process of learning. And technology is only part of the solution. All the computers in the world won't make a difference without enthusiastic students, skilled and committed teachers, involved and informed parents, and a society that underscores the value of lifelong learning. (*op cit*, p.i)

Educational technology, like most other forms of technology, provides us with a range of tools that may be applied to solve problems and make our work easier. In developing new technologies, the better the designers understand the problems that need to be solved, the better the quality of the solutions they will achieve. It was in these terms that the ESE initiative excelled above all the others. The particularly strong emphasis placed upon the involvement of professional early years educators and of children themselves in the processes of design was a great strength. The importance of this kind of collaboration cannot be overemphasised.

Concern has often been expressed regarding the 'failure' of many teachers to fully apply ICT in their classrooms. This has been a significant theme that has run through the 2002-3 BECTa Research Conference's in the UK. BECTa's IMPACT study has shown that in UK, primary school pupils still have little experience of ICT beyond the English language curriculum. But rather than see this as a problem of the teachers, it might be wiser to examine the research evidence we have more closely. If we consider the possibility that it may be the design of the technology currently available that is partly the problem, then the decision of many teachers to limit their application may be entirely sensible. In the development of new technologies it is crucial that we draw upon the expertise of teachers. Teachers already know a great deal about what it is that 'works' in their classrooms, what they need is support in identifying the technologies that might be applied in solving these problems more effectively. As Heppell (1999) has argued, the mistake has often been to look at computers as *teaching machines* that teachers must learn to *operate*, rather than as *learning tools* that may be *judiciously* applied to achieve a multitude of pedagogic ends.

In these terms the achievements of the ESE projects have been substantial, and it is therefore inevitable that only a fraction of the achievements may be presented in the chapters that follow. They begin with an introductory overview that has been strongly informed by my involvement in the programme through my membership of the CHAT working group. A variety of issues are then presented in chapters written by members of the project teams. The book closes with a chapter by Lieslotte Van Lewen, who elaborates upon an important strand that runs throughout the text and that featured strongly in all the work conducted in the ESE programme: the involvement of young children themselves as co-designers.

John Siraj-Blatchford

Further details of the ESE projects including contact details may be found at:
http://www.i3net.org/schools/links.html

Chapter One

Don't be surprised by the future: the development of appropriate new learning technologies for young children

John Siraj-Blatchford
University of Cambridge
Faculty of Education

Peter Sellers has been quoted as saying that the problem with predicting the future is that it is like scratching yourself before you start to itch... The analogy works particularly well in the context of technological development, where tomorrows technology can be seen as determined by tomorrow's cultural and economic choices. But as we all know, a little bit of scratching often results in a lot more itching, and our awareness of tomorrow's technological choices are in part determined by the technological choices we are making today. While only a minority of all of the technological products that come to be produced survive the test of time and the marketplace, in competitive market societies, there is a sense in which we must accept that culturally we deserve those that do.

It hasn't only been historians and ecologists who have shown us that cultures will be judged by the technologies that they create. Our relationship with technology is actually symbiotic; what we *make* says who we are...and we *are* what we make! While technology education is rarely considered a citizenship issue, the fact is that in the process of making technological choices and applying the technologies around us we also change ourselves. The technologies we develop change the way we think, live, and even the ways in which we perceive ourselves.

For all these reasons it took both courage and foresight to direct the research and development efforts of the *Experimental School Environment* (ESE) initiative towards non-traditional curriculum objectives. In the current climate of international educational league tables and an emphasis upon the 'basic' educational skills of reading, writing and arithmetic it is admirable that the European Commission was prepared to use this opportunity to explore new learning futures for children. The declared aims of the ESE programme were to produce novel ICT-based tools or environments that would promote the development of:

- creativity and imagination, curiosity and the art of asking questions'
- various forms of expression
- taking initiative
- learning to learn, setting goals and being aware of progress
- sharing, group activity and learning in teams

The ESE funding initiative formed part of the intelligent information interfaces (i³) component of the European Commissions *Esprit* Long Term Research programme. The general aim of i³ has been to develop human-centred interfaces for people in their everyday activities. In applying these aims to early learning the authors of the call for proposals argued that:

> In order to gain the full potential of IT, it is important to complement the introduction of current technological solutions to schools today, with a longer term vision of the future. New ideas and new paradigms have to be explored that are not bound by today's solutions. Open and visionary approaches have to be tried out that make learning a richer, more effective and more relevant activity, and ultimately a more fulfilling one.

> To do so, both educational and technological aspects have to be encouraged to evolve together, aiming to result in useful learning tools and not simply an eclectic collection of 'gadgets'. To this end, the call explicitly encourages methodologies that intertwine learning and technological research in exploratory and iterative ways. (European Commission, 1997)

It was felt that children aged between 4 and 8 provided a particularly 'open, inquisitive, and creative' cross section of learners, who had not yet been 'conditioned' into the more traditional thinking and behavioural patterns of their elders. The call for proposals explicitly referred to the possibilities of taking a broader view of literacy to encompass the full range of social interactions and media. Proposers were encouraged to work in multi-professional collaborative teams to investigate new paradigms for learning that might provide 'richer, more effective and more relevant learning for young children' (*op cit*).

A number of concrete suggestions were referred to in the call for proposals:

- New types of portable or wearable devices, artefacts or installations, that support interaction with one or more senses

- Artefacts that are fun and enjoyable to use but at the same time have clear educational purpose

- Toys or games that can be manually constructed or deconstructed

- Environments that bridge differences between 'virtual' and 'real' objects and activities

- Systems that can reflect 'friendliness' or 'emotion' through a combination of visual images, symbols, tactile sensations or sounds

- Personal learning assistants that act as intelligent guides, growing and adapting to a child's needs, and helping establish learning goals

- Environments that make it easy for children (and teachers) to create and display messages, experiences or snippets of information, in a range of media that can be accessed and used by others

- New systems to enable the growth of collective knowledge created by children and teachers

- Installations designed to encourage collaboration, participation and sharing with other children and teachers

- Environments designed to extend to communities and help bridge between cultures

As in all such initiatives, the final shape of the programme was determined by the particular interests, values, imagination, skills, as well as the prior knowledge and understandings of both the research applicants who competed for the funds and of those peer and expert reviewers who collaboratively decided how to allocate them. The final result was to award the funding to ten projects. While the successful applications addressed a wide range of the issues and concerns that were identified, their work focused upon three major areas of learning: the development of *creativity, curiosity and expression; metacognition and 'learning to learn'; and collaboration, participation and sharing*. While much of the research and development carried out by the ESE projects bridged these three concerns in a number of ways, for the sake of clear analysis it will be in these terms that the following general discussion of the work will be set. The chapter concludes with a discussion of the potential influence of learning technologies on play.

1. *Creativity, curiosity and expression*

A good way to understand the development of young children's creativity is to consider it in terms of the development and manipulation of 'schemes'. For Piaget (1969) and other developmental psychologists, a scheme is an operational thought or 'scheme of action', but for our purposes it can be thought of simply as a recalled behaviour, the recollection of a single action or a sequence of actions.[2] To be creative, children need to acquire a repertoire of schemes, and they also need the playful disposition to try out these schemes in new contexts. They may express these verbally, in their mind's eye, or in the material world. In fact young children are naturally curious and learn many of their schemes vicariously; they also spontaneously imitate a wide range of the schemes provided by adults and other children. In their fantasy play, young children quite naturally separate objects and actions from their meaning in the real world and give them new meanings. They should be encouraged to communicate these creative representations because it is in this way that their powers of expression and abstraction may be developed more generally. Educators may also encourage the discovery of schemes, and provide explicit models for the children to follow in their play.

Creativity, curiosity and expression provided a particular focus for three of the ESE projects; POGO, Today's Stories, and Caress. Because of their imagination and fantasy children will take schemes from one context and play them out in another. In the ESE projects technology was applied to support this process further and to help them communicate their achievements (expressions/ narratives/performances) to others.

The aim of the POGO project was to facilitate the creative process by providing a set of intuitive and child-friendly 'tools' that would empower the children to manipulate familiar objects, sounds and behaviours on screen. The technology built upon children's spontaneous urge to breath life into inanimate objects such as cuddly toys, dolls and plastic figures and animals, and to make up stories about their interactions. Narratives could be collaboratively developed around the children's favorite toys, pictures and sounds, and the children could feature themselves in their stories. The transformation of the concrete objects from the real world into a virtual story world was accomplished with active tools that were fully integrated so that they 'disappeared' in much the same way as paper and pencil is taken for granted in the process of writing. The tools included 'cards' that hold digital images, sounds or video clips, and a beamer (projector) base unit that incorporated an audio recording device, a wireless video camera and editing consol. The beamer provided the children with a means of saving their media into the cards and also of reading them onto a projection screen. Similarly wireless handheld 'torches' and 'boxes' provides alternative means of exploring, manipulating, and editing the contents of the cards. The children could thus independently construct multimedia narratives, activating images and/or related sounds simply by dropping the cards into a 'bucket' close to the screen.

Today's Stories aimed to support the development of children's social, communicative and emotional skills. A 'wearable' audio-visual recording technology (KidsCam) was used to document their own and other children's everyday activities. A 'Magic Mirror' provided a tangible interface that enabled the children to review and manipulate these episodes. The recordings also provided a means of reflecting and learning from other children's perspectives on their activities. By operating the Magic Mirror touch screen the children annotate the episodes, and could relate them to those experienced by other children. The Today's Stories technology was also developed to support individual and collective story authoring and the stories produced in collaboration with educators supported educational goals related to social and behavioural development. The edited multimedia files can also be linked to other materials for a variety of pedagogical purposes.

The CARESS project was designed to enable young children with special educational needs to learn and develop physical and cognitive skills by interacting with a responsive sound environment. Based around existing new technology, the Soundbeam converts physical movement into sound, and can be programmed so that a slow movement in the beam will be much quieter than a fast movement. The children's control over the sound is intuitive, interactive and exploratory and this motivates and empowers imagination and expression. Trials have shown that the Caress technology can improve the mobility of children with severe disabilities, and often leads to an 'awakening', heightened facial and vocal expression, body awareness and experience of joy.

2. *Metacognition and Learning to Learn*

The Concise Dictionary of Psychology defines metacognition as: having knowledge or awareness of one's own cognitive processes (Statt, 1998). 'Metacognition' thus describes the intellectual processess more commonly referred to in these pages as 'reflections'. Metacognition has been associated with effective learning in numerous contexts (Larkin, 2000) and the concept has been applied by educators seeking to design effective pedagogy. There is a general consensus that metacognition develops as the individual finds it necessary to describe, explain and justify their thinking about different aspects of the world to others (Perner *et al*, 1994; Pelligrini, Galda, and Flor, 1996; Lewis *et al*, 1996). The progress children make thus depends crucially upon their interactions with peers and adults, and upon the quality of their social, cultural and linguistic environment. Many psychologists believe that metacognitive knowledge and skills can also be taught and that this can make a dramatic difference in achievement. Initially, most programs designed to enhance metacognitive knowledge and skills were at the college level, but in recent years programs have appeared at the levels of secondary and even of early primary school education. (Roberts and Erdos, 1993; Smith, 1994; Brenna, 1995; Talizina, 1999; Lompsher, 1999, Larkin, 2000). For many 4 year-olds the first step towards developing such an understanding may be in the development of the concept that others hold representations of the world that are at variance with their own. For most children such a 'theory of mind' develops at about 41/2 years (Tan-Niam *et al*, 1999). Unsurprisingly research shows that children's pretend play becomes reciprocal and complementary at about the same time (Howes and Matheson, 1992). Research has established that a child with a 'theory of mind' is able to understand that other people have minds of their own, that they have their own understandings and motivations, and that they usually act according to their beliefs even when those beliefs are mistaken. It has also been argued (e.g. Kane, 1994; Slomskowski and Dunn, 1996) that the management of play 'through visual orientation, engagement with props/partner and topic maintenance' have also served to help children understand others' mental intentions and thoughts in shared play (Tan-Niam *et al*, 2000, p. 100). The implication is that play of this kind may support the child's metacognitive development and accordingly a study was developed to apply CCTV technology to encourage it (Siraj-Blatchford, J. and Siraj-Blatchford, 2002). Although the findings of this first study were disappointing, the subject undoubtedly warrants further study. A wide range of electronic toys may have such potential and before we turn to those developed for these purposes in the ESE projects it is useful to consider those currently on the market.

Most readers will be familiar with some of the 'intelligent' toys that have entered the domestic market in recent years but the following are offered as two typical examples of the genre:

> *Furby Babies* (Tiger Electronics, 1999) have a vocabulary of more that 800 words. They communicate with other Furby Babies, and they wiggle their ears, blink their eyes and move their lips, as well as 'talking' in response to movement and petting.

> *Super Poo-Chi* (Tiger Electronics, 2000) is an interactive puppy that sings, lies down, offers a paw and sits in response to voice commands, its bone and to touch. In a number of ways Super Poo-Chi behaves like a real dog: he communicates with other Robo-Chi(tm) 'pets', and his eyes display his 'emotions'.

Turkle (2000) has dubbed toys of this kind 'relational artefacts' because children often emotionally relate to them and treat them as 'sort of alive'. Toys such as these present themselves as having affective states of their own and they pose important questions about child development, about how adults and children think about life, and about the kind of relationships it is appropriate to have with a machine:

> Through their experiences with virtual pets and digital dolls (Tamagotchi, Furby, Amazing Ally), a generation of children are learning that some ob-

jects require (and promise) emotional nurturance. Adults, too, are encountering technology that attempts to meet their desire for personalised advice, care and companionship (help wizards, intelligent agents, AIBO, Matsushita's forthcoming Tama). Turkle (2000)

There is every indication that the future of computational technology will include many relational artefacts that have feelings, life cycles and moods; that reminisce, and have a sense of humour; which say that they love us and appear to expect us to love them back. Screen based software such as Mindscapes Babyz are already employing sophisticated voice recognition software to provide what the promoters refer to as 'virtual life'. These artefacts and applications raise significant new questions about how children approach the question of what is alive? As Turkle (2000) argues, the dynamic between a person and an emotionally interactive, evolving, caring machine is quite different from the relationship one might have with another person, or a pet, or even a cherished inanimate object.

There are a great many research questions to be explored in this context but one of the most significant features of many of these toys is that their behaviour has been programmed to 'develop' as they apparently 'learn' from their play with the child. In fact the 'learning' in this respect is more apparent than real. In developing their own robotic toy the *éTui* project team initially set about exploring with children, teachers and parents, a wide range of existing interactive toys. They found that the children were often strongly motivated by the characterisations and the aural and tactile experience of playing with the toys but the éTui team found the programming weak in terms of 'editing', 'storing' and 'revisiting' of instructions. They also found that children were disappointed when toys were unable to do what they claimed to do. The Furby was marketed with the clear implication that it could learn but they found that all it did was to reveal more of its pre-programmed (English rather than 'Furbish') responses over time. In chapter three reference is made to the ethical challenge that the project team took up in finding a balance in providing an intellectually honest and engaging robotic toy that could do more to support children's emerging awareness of learning.

The term 'éTui' was taken from the pan-European word used to denote a small tool container such as a that used to hold spectacles, pencils etc. and the central aim of the project team was to develop a set of tools for 'learning about learning'. The robotic toy produced is programmed by its environment, encouraging children to adapt the environment to explore and to reflect upon the toy's behaviour within it. The éTui robot can also learn, and this encourages children to reflect upon that learning, with the added benefit that this may well support them in considering their own learning.

In programming a robot to behave in certain ways, children have to see the problem from the robot's perspective. They have to *decentre*, adopting a body-centred system of reference which Papert (1980) termed 'body syntonicity'. This was a feature of the *Children in Choros and Chronos* (C3) project reported on more fully below. It also featured in the *Constructing with Atoms and Bits* (CAB) project, where the project team worked with children and teachers from Reggio Emelia in Italy to develop a range of appropriate robotic construction applications using a version of LEGO MindStorms, especially adapted for use by 5 and 6 year olds. As we see in chapter six, this was a pioneering project that motivated and empowered one group of children at Reggio Emelia's Villetta infant school to give a branch that had fallen from a tree after a heavy snow fall 'another kind of life'. Chioccariello, Manca and Sarti describe programming as a Pygmalion which provides the scientist with simulations, the poet with expressive fictions and the designer with dynamic modelling tools. For the 4 to 8 year olds they worked with, the robotic sub-assemblies or 'behaving objects' they developed empowered them as tangible object programmers. They argue that this early experience of programming has the potential of sharpening their thinking, fostering their creativity and enhancing their self-expression. This was pioneering work and the digital sound recorder bricks they describe even have possibilities for younger children.

The particular focus of the *PUPPET* development team was in socio-dramatic fantasy or make-believe play where children pretend on their own or interact, communicate and co-operate with others. The team applied activity theory, and the role of externalisation in cognitive development was also of special interest. Consequently, the specific cognitive benefits to the individual child of both individual and collaborative activities, as well as the roles of objects in supporting them were identified in the research.

The project created a novel inhabited virtual environment platform for educational purposes which was demonstrated and tested as a Farm Scenario. A dramaturgical framework, the 'Black Sheep Scenario' was developed within which the children were able to navigate and explore the virtual farm and the behaviour of the autonomous agents (farmer/animals) that inhabited it. The children could also choose any of the actors as avatar, and hence become present in the virtual world and interact with the other actors. The children were therefore able to act in a variety of roles within the puppet theatre:

- as an *audience* who actively navigated the virtual space, watching the interactions between the autonomous agents, trying to work out their goals and motivations

- as *improvising actors*, viewing and influencing the unfolding narrative as participants

- as *scriptwriters* recording inventive and humorous sounds for the agents or avatar

- as *editors* reflecting upon and re-recording the sounds recorded while playing with PUPPET as scriptwriter

The variety of roles that are taken by the children in this application clearly have direct relevance to the issue of 'theory of mind' and metacognition. In encouraging children to reflect upon their own motivations and those of other children, the Today's Stories project also has considerable potential. Many of the projects considered below in terms of collaboration, participation and sharing have similar qualities and possibilities. For example, one objective of the *Children in Chros and Chronos (C3) project* was also to provide a range of learning activities that involved the children in the acting out of stories involving people's belief systems, aspirations, intentions.

3. *Collaboration, participation and sharing*

The *PLAYGROUND* project aimed to apply ToonTalk and in OpenLogo in constructing virtual playgrounds within which children could develop their own games. This set the six to eight year-olds that they worked with firmly in the role of games producers rather than mere consumers. The project focused its analysis strongly on the ways in which the children were able to appreciate, develop and adapt the rules. The project has shown how the tension between rule based play and creativity can be resolved at an early age in the process of collaboration and the formalisation of rule systems.

One of the most intriguing findings may be that the online collaboration that was facilitated by the children sharing their games with 'critical friends' on the internet supported them in the process of developing (or expressing) system/formal rules as opposed to narrative accounts. It seems that in the absence of face-to-face communication and collaboration the children found it necessary to formalise their thinking. Similar processes may well be involved in the process of young children's online collaborative drawing using Microsoft's Netmeeting. This was a Portuguese (Portalegre) initiative identified in the DATEC (http://www-datec. educ.cam.ac.uk) project and reported upon more fully in Siraj-Blatchford, J. and Siraj-Blatchford, I. (2004).

The Playground team found that even quite late in the project some children were still trying to weave extremely complex scenarios into their games, scenarios that were beyond their own capability to realise or even the capability of the programming system. This was a familiar problem for primary school teachers in the early days of implementing the national curriculum for Design and Technology in the UK. Many teachers at that time interpreted the organisation of the curriculum attainment targets as a prescription of pedagogy. The first attainment targets referred to the need for children to learn to identify a design problem or opportunity and then to develop a design solution. Taken as a curriculum starting point such an approach invited children to *invent* when their skills and knowledge were still only sufficient to support them in the more modest design and technological activities of *adaptation* and *modification* (Siraj-Blatchford and MacLeod-Brudenell, 1999).

The main objective of the *Children in Chros and Chronos* (C3) project was to develop game-like collaborative activities that promoted children's spatio-temporal awareness and cognition while developing specific skills like map reading. In the light of the foregoing discussion it may be significant that C3's 'Treasure Hunt in the Castle' trial involved six year olds in the collaborative development of an treasure map where they were provided with an existing map that was incomplete rather than providing them with a blank sheet of paper.

The C3 project applied Global Positioning System (GPS) technology in creating activities that demanded sophisticated communication between two groups of children. Two collaborating teams were involved, with one located at a base workstation that ran the activity software, and the other team moving around the activity environment carrying a high precision (+/- 1m) GPS device and communicating with the base team via walkie-talkies. The technology provided a means by which the base-team were able to observe (in real time) the exact path taken by the mobile team. The key technological challenge was to integrate the GPS technology is such a way as to allow the children at the base station to edit and investigate their spatial representation in collaboration with the children moving around in the area represented. While completing their maps the children were able to use the walki-talkies to discuss what the important landmarks were and what icons might be used to represent them. In their final report the project team reported on the success that the children had in establishing the correspondent relationships between the representation and referent spaces. The children also found the need 'to use and discuss frames of reference, symbolisation (uniform coding, perspective, iconicity), the relative positioning of symbols on the plane, accuracy in the placement of the symbols on the map and correspondence between the real space and its representation'.

There is general agreement among developmental psychologists and educationalists that collaboration is especially important in the early years. When children share 'joint attention', 'learn to share' and/or 'engage jointly' in activities this provides a significant cognitive challenge (Light and Butterworth, 1992). The value of ICT in supporting collaborative learning has also been demonstrated (Crook, 1994; Dillenbourg, 1999). But successful collaboration does not automatically occur simply whenever we bring children together to share the same computer. As Crook (1994) has shown, teachers need to orchestrate collaborative interactions if there are to be learning gains.

The KidStory project provides valuable messages for ICT designers and also for educational practitioners. Many of the findings have immediate implications for practitioners who may already have access to large displays and multiple input devices and these are reported upon fully in chapter five. Designers and research students will also find the methodological accounts that are provided of particular value and a number of problems and questions are identified for further study. KidStory aimed to develop collaborative storytelling technologies. In doing so they initially extended the University of Maryland's KidPad software, which provided a means by which a variety of tools could be employed to create/draw story objects and to link these elements together to create narratives. When the children zoom in on individual story object to work on it the KidStory extensions have allowed them to work in pairs operating multiple mice and other tools on the same screen. The project has also developed more physical and tangible interfaces to support the collaboration of groups in the classroom and the evidence suggests that these have supported some significant improvements in the quality of the children's stories. The final interface design involved the integration of a number of technologies into a 'magic carpet'. These included arrays of pressure mats and the use of physical props associated with either barcode or video tracking technologies that allowed them to navigate their stories.

The main aim of the *NIMIS* project was to develop a classroom for early learners which featured a synergy between social, educational and technological factors. This is described in chapter two by Cooper and Brna. Their 'Classroom of the Future' was achieved through employing dedicated software in computer integrated classrooms that have featured the use of large touch sensitive display screens, and the use of smaller Wacom workstations with pen-based input. The software implemented in NIMIS has included *Today's Talking Typewriter*, the creative writing software *T'rrific Tales*, and the 3D story creation software *Teatrix*. Intelligent agents (Louisa and Maria) have also been developed to support the children's activity.

The evidence has shown that *NIMIS* has supported the development of emergent literacy in different ways. The technology supported the teachers in providing more opportunities for collaboration through structured shared tasks, and to support more spontaneous interactions involving pair work, group work, and whole class collaboration. The children have therefore been given more opportunities to collaborate, and to take on leadership roles that build their confidence and self-esteem.

The use of speech synthesis has been particularly successful and this was found to give children greater control over their learning of both phonics, whole words, phrases, and stories. The children were able to re-read their stories in *T'rrific Tales* without adult support. They were also empowered to find their own words in the software word bank. They were able to copy the spellings into their own story and were often heard sounding out the words in the process. As Cooper and Brna note, in the absence of the technology the volume of writing activity that was observed would simply have been impossible in the classroom with one adult to 23 children.

Conclusions

While writing this overview chapter I have been struck by the relevance of recent work by van Oers (1999). Writing from an Activity theory perspective, van Oers adopts a conception of play in the early childhood as being a 'leading activity' (Leontiev, 1981; Oerter, 1993). Such leading activities are seen as a driving force in the child's development of new forms of motivation and action, and play and imitation are considered primary contexts for representational and symbolic behaviour. Roleplay is therefore considered central to the processes of learning in the early years. As van Oers (1999) has suggested, when children consciously reflect upon the relationship between their 'pretend' signs and 'real' meanings they are engaged in a form of semiotic activity that provides a valuable precursor to new learning activities (p. 278). In discussing the transition from play to learning activity, Carplay and van Oers (1993) argue that:

> ...learning activity must be fostered as a new special form of play activity. As a new quality emerging from play activity, it can be argued that learning activity has to be conceived as a language game in which negotiation about meanings in a community of learners is the basic strategy for the acquisition of knowledge and abilities. (van Oers, 1999, p. 273)

This approach might be considered implicit in emergent literacy and numeracy practices where educators specifically encourage children to recognise the value of using symbols to represent and quantify artifacts. A great deal can be done to promote these processes in the wider play context and new forms of play might usefully be developed in relation to the new technologies (Siraj-Blatchford, J and I., forthcoming, 2004).

In Chapter 4 Hoyles and Noss describe a situation where the children in London designed a tropical island scene and sent it to their in Swedish research partners with no game narrative to support it. To satisfy the needs of their critical friends they then thought it necessary to add system rules but found that this changed their intended (game) narrative. It may therefore be the case that the process of expressing player narratives (in this case motivated by the need for communication) represents a valuable first stage or prerequisite in the identification of system rules. Children in the C3 project were required to communicate to other children in a similar way and children have also been engaged in providing narrative accounts of play in the *POGO, Today's Stories* and KidStory projects. In the C3 project the research team noted the need for teachers to provide the children with initial support in realising the 'consequences' of loose communication or miscommunication. Subsequent efforts to achieve 'communicational rigour' seemed to come about through the children's own attempts to reach their joint goals. As the team say in their final report:

> The issue of collaboration for joint construction as a vehicle for meaning generation is interesting and warrants further study, particularly with respect to the ways in which a social mode of learning can be enhanced by the representational tools and overall focus to this type of activity.

Chapter Two

A classroom of the future today

Bridget Cooper and Paul Brna
School of Informatics,
Northumbria University
United Kingdom

The Context

Of all the experimental school environments (ESE) projects, NIMIS (Networked Interactive Media in Schools) was most closely aligned with children in their normal classroom environment. NIMIS featured a collaboration between three research groups and their partner schools and one commercial firm interested in projection equipment over the period October 1998 to October 2000 inclusive. The primary goal, as originally expressed, was to research the provision of digital media management in the primary school classrooms of tomorrow. The project focussed on the support of literacy including learning to read, learning to write and the development of narrative skills, as well as having a strong focus on helping children develop their capability for seeing the other's point of view through activities designed to foster both second and third person perspectives.

The work described here was primarily carried out at the Computer Based Learning Unit at Leeds University together with their partner school, a county primary school in Yorkshire (Glusburn). Inevitably, the work was strongly influenced by our collaboration with the team at INESC (Lisbon, Portugal) and the COLLIDE group at Duisburg University, Germany and their associated schools. At Glusburn, a 'classroom of the future' was designed and installed incrementally. The end result was a local intranet featuring a suite of networked PCs placed in a classroom for Year One children (five to six year olds). The suite used high quality PC technology and included a scanner, black and white printer, colour printer, loudspeakers, headphones, WACOM touch sensitive tablets and a large 50 inch touchscreen supplied by MediaWorld, the commercial partner in the project. The Leeds team's software sits 'on top' of a Windows-NT environment and provides a functionality which supports highly collaborative interactions over the classroom intranet. This configuration was very similar to the ones in the associated schools – Kirchstrasse school near Duisburg and the O Nosso Sonho school in Lisbon.

In the Glusburn context, the classroom in which the NIMIS hardware and software was located had 26 children from five to six years old for the first year of the project and 23 for the second year. This Year One class was shared between two teachers. The school itself is rural, and has about 350 children enrolled. Before the NIMIS project began, the teachers in the selected Year One class were able to use a single PC running Windows 95 to allow children access to a number of commercial stand alone software packages. Children are taught in classes, small groups or individually, from time to time, according to individual needs, within the framework of the National Curriculum for England and Wales. At the start of the project, Glusburn was considered quite advanced in terms of its ICT development as a primary school with a bank of software and substantial hardware and an open and positive attitude to the use of ICT. However there were considerable staff training needs, and the ICT literacy of the staff was very uneven.

Turning to the support for literacy, the National Curriculum for England and Wales had just specified in some detail what activities must take place in the literacy hour, and how long these activities should last. For the period of the NIMIS project, the curriculum did not allow much time for creative writing and learning to construct narrative – with story telling used as a vehicle by teachers for a number of different issues (vocabulary, spelling, punctuation, etc.). This provides a brief but hopefully sufficient background to introduce the context in which the work took place. But first we explain the approach taken throughout the project to support children.

Theoretical Underpinning

The NIMIS project, like the other ESE projects, was intended to promote a range of values which go beyond a narrow understanding of education as being curriculum centred, and sought to ensure that technology was harnessed to help children enjoy learning by providing them with social, emotional and cognitive support via the sensitive incorporation of various technologies into the classroom context.

According to Vygotsky, cognitive development is, at root, embedded in social relations: 'all the higher functions originate as actual relations between human individuals' (Vygotsky, 1978, p57). Such relations between human beings are not only influenced by cognitive factors but also by instinctual and emotional elements, which give depth and meaning to learning, provide motivation, raise self-esteem and improve the ability to feel for and understand others. Positive relationships where trust is created and success achieved provide the security for children to make those leaps into the unknown which new learning, of whatever nature, entails. A positive, nurturing, and enabling atmosphere which supports all children provides the model for their own personal development and relationships with others. We believe that flexible classrooms designed to meet children's needs, to encourage a wide range of interaction and collaboration, to enable the co-construction of ideas, presentation of ideas and subsequent reflection, can help to support and nurture the emotional, social and intellectual development of children.

The position is therefore taken that the social, emotional and cognitive are all interrelated in quite complicated ways (Damasio, 1994; Goleman, 1995), and that therefore the design of a classroom of tomorrow is simultaneously the design of an environment for promoting useful social interactions, promoting the learning of reading, writing, spelling and for providing emotional support. However, since all three elements intertwined, we emphasise that there are grounds for believing that getting the emotional support wrong will prevent most, if not all, children from achieving the highest educational levels. Excellence in teaching and learning has often been related by researchers to the quality of teacher/pupil relationships and the school and classroom ambience (Aspy, 1972; Kyriacou, 1986).

A major focus of the work in Leeds was therefore to ensure that the classroom ambience was 'designed' as far as possible to provide an emotionally supportive environment to help children learn through activities such as creative story writing, deploying the advanced hardware and software at our disposal in as sensitive a manner as possible.

Within this environment, we hoped that children would be encouraged to practice and develop their creative story writing skills. Implicit in the nature of creativity is an ability to be open to new ideas, to make connections between differing ideas and to try new and exciting forms of self-expression (Bryson, 1999). The challenge for teachers and also for educational software is to make the children feel secure and confident enough to make the leaps into the creativity involved in story writing and indeed in any form of learning.

The teacher and the software must offer just enough structure and intervention to allow children to progress securely and successfully and offer enough stimulation and variety of approach so that they can establish creative links (Edwards and Springate, 1995). Recent understanding of how the brain works, coupled with detailed understanding about the teaching and learning process (Cooper *et al,* 2000) led us to believe that creative writing could be supported and encouraged through software such as that which we eventually developed (*T'rrific Tales*). Firstly by the structure and content of the software and also by the use of an explicit empathic agent, which was intended to encourage and support children in their tasks either individually or collaboratively (Cooper and Brna, 2001).

Stories are embedded in every aspect of our lives (Berger, 1997), from the tales we tell of our day at work or school to the stories we tell of our worst and greatest moments, embroidering the mundane with excitement and charging the routine with emotion. Narrative is a fundamental aspect of the human experience. The human connections made in stories through emotional cues echo those leaps in the brain which are also closely triggered by emotional responses. Some of our most creative moments and our most lateral thinking happen when our rational brain is resting and the unconscious, intuitive aspects are allowed to mull freely (Hesten, 1995; Claxton, 1997) when we open ourselves up in a highly receptive way to deep and diverse thinking. According to Greenfield our human creativity may well be nurtured by the leaps made between the complementary but very different halves of the brain (Greenfield, 2000). Damasio (1994) and Goleman (1996) emphasise the emotional nature of decision-making, and Noddings (1984) highlights the receptiveness and openness needed for caring behaviour. It seems that the empathic approach needed for stimulating personal growth and development may be similar to that needed to enable creativity. The combination of security plus stimulation and receptivity to different ideas creates a fertile ground for the creative imagination.

In terms of assessing the impact of our approach, it is the inter-related nature of learning and the myriad daily interactions between individuals and groups which creates the complexity and makes it particularly difficult to evaluate learning in the constantly changing dynamics of the classroom. The nature of the hidden curriculum in the classroom (Rutter *et al,* 1979; Department of Education and Science, 1989) can also subvert the more visible and tangible aspects of learning and is likely to confound aspirations of any straightforward evaluation. Differing social and academic relationships between a child's peers and other adults in school can make each child's learning experience unique and therefore particularly difficult to assess.

Design and Evaluation

There are four key areas for which NIMIS was involved in developing the concept of the classroom of the future, and hence interested in evaluating as part of the design process: the whole classroom context; collaborative activities; interfaces and how they support learning; and literacy development. The methodology for the design drew on the notion of informant design (Scaife *et al,* 1997) and an approach derived from Carroll's participatory design methodology (Carroll and Rosson, 1992; Chin *et al,* 1997). Carroll's methodology is one of several participatory design approaches, and is organised around the identification and exploration of key scenarios. It exploits a form of design rationale known as claims analysis. The claims concept was extended to incorporate the pedagogical intentions underlying the design, and this revised form was termed pedagogical claims analysis – see Cooper and Brna (2000) for more details about claims. As a consequence of the use of a form of participatory design, both the design of the classroom and its evaluation were deeply intertwined with the initial claims being revised and validated throughout the formative prototyping phase.

Methodological Issues

This evaluation is based mainly on data recorded in the NIMIS classroom at Glusburn school over the academic year from 1999 to 2000 but includes some data gathered in the three months before this as the classroom was being set up, and in the pre-NIMIS classroom before any equipment arrived. There were 23 children in this year 1 class (5 and 6 year olds) for the academic year and there was only one teacher except for a few sessions per week attended by parent helpers or classroom assistants. However there are two different teachers for the class, one teaching Monday to Wednesday and the other Thursday to Friday.

The teachers have the National Curriculum to adhere to and well-defined teaching methodologies for the core aspects of the curriculum. Conducting research into anything innovatory whilst working within the NC framework is difficult for everyone concerned. Teachers are struggling to complete all the NC tasks and administration without the extra work and tasks of a research project. The school day is so packed with activities that there is little room for manoeuvre. It is a credit to the teachers involved in this project that they found time to write diaries, read documents, attend meetings, be interviewed and interact with researchers while carrying out their normal, demanding teaching tasks. However the strength of this research is that it reflects the real use of hardware and software in a real year one classroom environment with substantial amounts of data from a variety of sources

This evaluation also refers to data and analysis from mini-projects conducted by individuals within the NIMIS framework. One was a project looking at how the NIMIS classroom affected teaching in the numeracy hour, another looked specifically at collaboration issues, another considered whether teaching practices were changed by the introduction of the NIMIS classroom, and another compared

Figure 1: The classroom mid-transformation

the ICT skills of the NIMIS class with the other year one class. In terms of the originally planned data collection, we have data from ongoing diaries from the two teachers, conversations and two lengthy interviews each. We have data from observations and video recordings over about forty hours of lesson time. We have story analysis of eighty-two stories written using *T'rrific Tales*, coupled with analysis of pen and paper assessments. We have test data for reading ages and NC levels for September, Easter and the end of the summer term. We have computer logs for all the later eleven sessions using *T'rrific Tales*. We have three interviews with about a third of the children each time, plus field notes and videos which capture many of their comments and reactions to the classroom and software, and reflections on the software by the children who helped design it in the previous year. This range of data allows us to see the classroom and the software from different perspectives to achieve a rich and complex understanding of the process.

The Whole Classroom

The classroom in Glusburn was eventually equipped with a large back-projected touchscreen, seven high specification Pentium II PCs, six WACOM PL-300 LCDs with touch sensitive displays using pen-based input, scanner, colour printer, greyscale printer, and a digital camera. The touchscreen was selected for both whole class teaching and children working alone or together. The touch-screen allowed children to use their fingers to drag objects, double click on an icon to launch an application and to work with drawing packages such as Dazzle directly with their fingertips (Figure 1 shows the classroom nearing the end of its transformation with two monitors still needing to be replaced with WACOMs).

A major design goal was to make sure that the computers did not impede normal face to face communication between children and their teachers, hence the selection of the low profile WACOM PL-300s. Additionally, furniture was selected for the classroom that allowed children to work round a table together. Six workstations were located around an octagonal table selected from a commercial vendor. The PCs were placed out of sight so that only the WACOM PL-300s, pens, keyboards and headphones were visible. From the evaluation work it became evident that the large screen and the network around the octagonal table were used daily and for long periods (up to five hours per day) and were well embedded into daily teaching and learning in this Year One classroom.

The enthusiasm, engagement in and enjoyment of the NIMIS classroom continued unabated, despite our early fears of it perhaps losing its novelty value as the months passed. Both children and teachers were highly complimentary about the facilities it provided and it was used voluntarily for many hours each day and across the curriculum right until the end of the academic year, as well as being used with the *T'rrific Tales* software in specific sessions.

A comment from a child who was asked about having the classroom for a year was typical:

> 'Well, it's rather very good, because it's... so good to have... new techwork... network... every day to go in the computers, 'cos I really love T'rrific Tales.'

Another child, asked why she liked it, answered for her classmates too:

> '...because it's really nice and people love it. They always want to play with it all the time... it makes me feel happy and feels nice'

In the final interviews the teachers were still very pleased with the whole classroom and described it as 'wonderful', 'a perfect world' and said 'I wouldn't be without it'.

Reflecting on the children's attitude they echoed the children's feelings, 'they love it... and at the end of the day they love to go there (on the computers), they still have the same amount of enthusiasm (as at the start)'.

The teachers explained how the classroom helped with their teaching because of the flexibility provided by the large screen and table of small WACOM tablets. They also appreciated the range of software and told us that they could easily integrate the computers into their teaching in a very natural way. One teacher explained how other teachers in the school, who were wary of the NIMIS classroom looked at it sometimes as if it might be some sort of burden and that they just didn't realise 'that it could help towards making a much easier life for you – it fits in as another tool – it's totally integrated. It's natural, it's spontaneous.'

We had no negative responses about the classroom from children or teachers although the first few weeks with the new five year olds in September 1999 were quite demanding because they all found it so new. The teachers had been keen to use the equipment all day but they realised they needed to move more slowly with the new class. However by the first half term the children were much more competent and relatively independent.

There is definitely a sense from the teachers and the children's final interviews that a good helping atmosphere operated in the class. There is evidence to show that collaborative and helping behaviours were encouraged and that children had opportunities to gain confidence in front of each other and also by explaining things to each other. In this sense the helpful ambience we had hoped to create did appear to be realised. Building self-esteem and through that the ability to take other perspectives in such a collaborative and communicative environment was an aim of the NIMIS project. However both the teachers and children were probably also influenced by the 'extra people in the classroom at times' (Hawthorn effect). One teacher specifically mentioned that she thought people in the class had had an effect:

> Well it's a difficult one that, because I don't know what they would have been like without the machines, so I can't say whether they would have got more self esteem and confidence. They have certainly got confidence in using the machine, they've got confidence in demonstrating the machines ... I think they've become quite sort of blasé about all the people, that's given them self esteem, all the visitors. You know, they're used to sort of talking to lots of strangers, and they'll take this in their stride and not worry about this at all. But again, this is an excellent class, it's a superb class.

Apparently the computers did not have a negative effect on children's behaviour but the two teachers said in the final interview that:

> Well, with each other, maybe... they actually are great because if someone runs into trouble they don't become embarrassed or belittled by it, and there's always someone to go over and generally help them because they want to support them, they've got that really good team thing going there, really good... they're not at all, I've never heard any of banter... there's a lot of support, and I think they feel quite proud, I mean they definitely do.

> They are fairly co-operative and helpful to each other all the time, I mean some classes are better than others, this particular class are very nice, and

they have been... you know, they help each other when they are doing written work, they help each other when they are doing activities work, and they help each other when they on the computer, there's no doubt about that...

The teachers also felt that the classroom had an effect on learning, though it wasn't always easy to articulate what and why. One teacher explained how she hadn't thought computers were very relevant but now she said she thought differently about it because of the set-up in the NIMIS classroom, which was different to having just one or two machines in the corner or a suite of computers in a different part of the school.

The computers in the classroom, yes because you can have a scenario like I have got, a perfect world, then you can see that it makes huge changes in the development of the children, it's another learning tool.

Collaboration

We have looked at factors which support different forms of collaboration and what those differing forms of collaboration might be. There are many different definitions of collaboration and we take the position that we need to use a whole range of forms of collaboration to enhance communication and learning. Varying the ways of working allows for both personal and shared reflection and differing levels of intensity of collaboration and different degrees of timeliness of support and independence.

In the NIMIS classroom we have seen collaboration in large and small groups around the large screen, sometimes with a teacher participant and sometimes without. We have seen collaboration around the octagonal table, sometimes structured, sometimes spontaneous, in pairs, threes, or fours, sometimes with interventions from interested temporary collaborators, sometimes from casual passers-by. We have seen discussion and support across the table and also from teachers and researchers for both individuals, pairs and larger groups.

It seems that all these forms of interaction occurring as they do at different times and with different types of exchange, are significant in children's learning. Whether the dialogue was centred around creating stories, around technical issues or around social and personal issues, all these facets are part and parcel of learning and need valuing according to the function they perform. There is also considerable evidence from videos, diaries and interviews that the combination of hardware and interactive software which allows shared viewing, listening and creating of multi-media stories supports collaboration and writing conferences. Children can be seen helping each other to write stories on both large and small screens and they discuss what to include and discard. They can edit and improve their work easily and this is confirmed by the data in the computer logs where children make many changes to their work. They can be seen reading each other's stories and taking an interest in what has been written, thus affirming their class-mates work and giving an alternative perspective. The collaborative tool in *T'rrific Tales* enabled children to send each other characters to include in each other's stories and the teachers have also used the large screen to write stories to-gether as a whole class and also for discussing the finer details of writing and reading in the literacy hour.

Certainly the NIMIS classroom seemed to offer a greater range of ways of work-ing and the facilities to enable that to happen. The shared workspaces large and small, the layout of the room and the facility to share ideas electronically all contribute to a greater variety of opportunities to communicate and interact and to share and preserve (if required) the results of that interaction. Children of 5 and 6, still developing their interpersonal skills and their understanding of themselves and their awareness of the needs of others (as indeed are many adults) need to have opportunities for a wide range of opportunities to interact, some of which are less demanding than others. This is especially so when the ratio of adults to child is such that adult intervention may be infrequent and the adult model of col-laboration unavailable at the point at which it is needed.

Videos and observations made of the classroom before and after the introduction of the NIMIS hardware and software have been analysed for quality of inter-action, engagement and control in classroom relationships to try and understand the nature and quality of different types of sessions and what they can tell us about the nature of collaboration in relation to learning, self-esteem and perspec-tive taking in the NIMIS classroom. These lessons included whole class sessions, individual working sessions and group working sessions. Coding the recorded interactions using a video coding scheme especially developed for the project (Cooper and Brna, 2000) has given insight into the quality of interactions and collaboration taking place in theNIMIS classroom. We understand that coding video is not always straightforward and it became apparent when observing class-rooms that the subtleties of interaction are complex and not always easy to identify and quantify. Nevertheless the complexity is what adds the depth to the understanding of such aspects of teaching and learning. Our video-coding scheme was developed and used for analysing all the videos involving literacy in the classroom and a few mathematics lessons.

With the arrival of the computers the children had frequent opportunities to work around a shared task in pairs and wider groups on both the large and small screens around the octagonal table – opportunities that they had not had before. They were also able to participate actively around the large screen as part of whole class activities. These two activities appeared to be qualitatively different from others in terms of the interpersonal skills needed, and the motivation created by the coming of the computers. The new activities led to high levels of engagement in collaborative situations and this has continued throughout the year with no lessening of enthusiasm. However, collaborative situations were not altogether unproblematic. When children had to negotiate who did what while working on a specific task together there were usually arguments about control. In the few instances where engagement faltered, the child who lost interest was always subject to a partner who dominated the control of the task and often did not interact well with them.

Even then the children often spent a long time (between 20-40 minutes) showing considerable interest in the task before they displayed their frustration at their lack of control. But the passive nature of their learning and any resentment building up about inequality might have had other undesirable effects. Working with an uncompromising and dominant partner in one episode later, one child modelled precisely the same dominant behaviour with another passive child. There was more evidence on the issue of collaboration from the children themselves and the teachers in the final interviews. Their answers plus the video evidence tend to suggest that children need to experience and prefer to experience a range of ways of working and that they need different levels of support at different times. Here is a typical child's comments when asked how she preferred to work:

> 'Sometimes with a partner, sometimes with a friend, sometimes on my own'

Another two explained the advantages of working with a friend, 'because sometimes they just have these great ideas and if I haven't got some ideas, maybe I can ask them'

> 'Yes we do help each other because, for example, if I was working on the computer and my friend came along, my friend would help me'

She went on to explain how learning passed from one friend to another:

> 'Because Hannah was the first one to discover how to get off and on problems (she means logging on and off), yes and then Jane... and then me'

And another child, asked about working around the table, said:

> 'If you get stuck you just go like this (mimes leaning over) and ask the other person what to do'

However problems with collaboration which were identified in the video analysis when incompatible personalities were put together were also understood by the children. One child articulated it in this way,

'Well, I do like it when I'm with my friends, but, yeah, I do like it with my friends, but if they aren't my friends we just fall out then I just argue a little bit and then we all become friends again.'

A teacher explained how the children preferred different ways of working at different times but often they chose to work collaboratively on the computers.

'...but if they are working on something that is more collaborative, something that needs more discussion, like (software program) they'll sit down together'

This also suggests that though the children think the software is fun the task can often be more demanding, which is why they need to collaborate. Getting the right balance between the level of task and the support available seems crucial to providing the best learning experience.

Interfaces

The initial enthusiasm about the touch screen, seemed to grow over the duration of the project. Used across the curriculum by teachers and pupils, it proved an excellent support for learning and was used daily. Video analysis of the touch screen being used by both pupils and teachers and the teacher diaries shows it is used in different ways, with a good deal of different software by both teachers and children. In at least three videos the expression 'It's magic' is used by children and teachers to describe the use of software on the large screen. This occurred in two maths lessons and in a video when children opened up their *T'rrific Tales* stories on the large screen, in order to present them to the class.

One teacher described how now she could remember little bits of the software that could reinforce or demonstrate particular things and how she could just find them and use them, even on the spur of the moment, beginning, perhaps with a little sequence which really helped the children to learn a maths concept, and then later reinforcing their learning in a slightly different way on a worksheet or by playing the game themselves on the small screens. They don't use the computers if it is not appropriate but wherever it is appropriate they use it, 'If it can be used it will be used.'

Both teachers recognised the benefits of the combination of the big screen and the small screens:

'...the big screen... it's more fun... it's not a boring blackboard, it's not a boring teacher going on and on... it's fun. You have all these games and at the same time they're learning it's nice to be able to provide that enormous amount of variety so it doesn't become staid and the computer software provides that variety'

They explained how they used the large screen as a teaching aid for introductions, discussions and recaps and the small screens for independent work. The large screen was particularly helpful for the literacy hour. The teachers rarely use the old easel now, but use the interactive board and store pre-prepared material or brainstorming sessions for later use. The interactive nature of the board helps to 'get them involved', as one teacher put it. The hardware has proved to be very popular with the children and more evidence of what they liked about the large screen came in the final interviews:

> '...because it's big and everyone can see. Even from the top of the building'

> 'You don't have to go like that (mimes moving the mouse) you just have to touch it with your finger..its really good and you can see most things'

In relation to the WACOM tablets and mouse pens, all the evidence from the videos, the teacher and children's interviews suggests that they have had plenty of chances to interact in different ways with these computers and other children and that they have been tremendously motivated by it and have gained self-confidence through it. The NIMIS children used the mouse for precision pinpointing (because sometimes the pen action needed to be repeated and wasn't absolutely accurate on the tiniest icons) but they used the pen for drawing and manipulating software. In the videos they can often be seen switching between different tools. The teachers preferred them to use a mixture because it built on their existing skills of both pen and pencil and the mouse (most use a mouse at home). It was felt that they needed experience with the mouse because they would not have this special equipment in subsequent years but will have to use a mouse. All the children said they liked the WACOMs and mouse pens. Of the mouse pens one child said:

> '...they're really good- you get to hold on like a pencil and pretend you're writing'

And another:

> Int: 'Lovely, what do you think about those WACOM tablets? Those little screens where you use the pen?'

> 'I like it because you don't have to use the mouse, and you can just pick up the pen and go like that, and sometimes some people work on others and they work on the other side sometimes.' (can use pen on any machine)

We were particularly pleased with the way the children used these devices quickly and collaboratively but think the angle and size of the WACOM screen makes a difference to the ease of use. We would probably aim to use larger WACOMs in a future project, possibly set into a flat table but keeping the octagonal or similar nature of the table set up. The children's initial response to the *T'rrific Tales* story writing software were extremely positive. The first time it was used, with only a few words of explanation, it only took a few seconds for children to begin to create story pictures. They enjoyed the software right away even without the support of the word banks and speech synthesis that were added later. They were enthusiastic and managed to write stories in pairs and individually. Creating simple stories with one picture and a little narrative was fairly straightforward as long as they had support with spelling from adults. Dragging and dropping the picture labels to help write the story proved popular and they used this well. As time passed some of the higher attaining children were able to write fairly long stories for five and six year olds with minimal support. Working in pairs and collaborating over a finished product proved more difficult than manipulating the interface. They also enjoyed using the collaborative tool and passing pictures to each other, to form the basis of a shared story.

The children continued to use the *T'rrific Tales* software enthusiastically right up until the end of the summer term in 2000. Their stories became longer and more elaborate, growing from just one to three or four scenes, in which characters from school and fantasy were creatively mixed and matched. They managed to write these stories quite easily in a range of ways – working as individuals, in pairs, groups of four and whole class stories around the large screen. The introduction of the word banks and speech synthesis produced new challenges and new excitement for the children. Though the later prototype was a complex piece of software and still did not have all the structure and support built into it that we would have liked by that stage, the children really enjoyed using it and used the word banks and phrases from the outset to create more elaborate and varied stories with appropriate pictures and vocabulary. They incorporated atmospheric titles and openings as well as story stirrers to produce rounded stories with creative plots. They used speech bubbles and thought bubbles to add different perspectives and dynamics to their stories and used the banks of common words to find spellings. The speech-synthesis allowed them to hear words and phrases and re-read their stories with less teacher support, and they could incorporate the language into their own linguistic banks.

Scaffolding is provided as the children learn vocabulary and story structures all the time they are using the software, which is not the case when they have to work entirely on their own. Some children do not have the raw material to draw on to create stories and *T'rrific Tales* helps by offering them suggestions. While children often struggle to re-read their stories because of spellings, the software allows them to re read much more of it and many words (though not all) have pictures to support understanding. We were concerned the children would not try to read the words for themselves, but they usually did read and listen and often repeated the words and phrases they heard or incorporated into their stories. They also share them with friends when they are working together and in the videos you can hear children repeating the phrases and words from the word banks out loud. None of this would be possible if the teacher was trying to get round all twenty three children to sound out words. The video evidence also testifies to the higher quality of interaction and learning offered by the teacher when they do look at children's work. But it is also noticeable that when pairs share a story adults also spend time supporting their social skills because of the problems that sharing creates.

Generally the word banks helped the children's writing and provided an area of support of that no single teacher can provide in a large class. They also offered a basis for discussion between children and further elaboration of ideas. The suggestions and tips, particularly, produced a big improvement on the usual openings. We hope to develop these hints with the help of the agent. Children listened to and thought about the story endings but didn't really incorporate them into stories. This was to be expected as the suggestions and examples given naturally didn't fit the stories the children had written. The suggestions required a high level of adaptation.

Literacy Development

The classroom was used throughout the 1999/2000 school year. After some initial use of the software in its first prototypical state from November to April, the children went on to use *T'rrific Tales* with the word banks and speech synthesis in twice weekly sessions for around three months to the end of July. Each session lasted from around half an hour to one and a half hours depending on the circumstances. Writing a story with *T'rrific Tales* was usually one of several options available to children in the afternoons. Other options included national curriculum activities, reading groups, story time and time with special needs assistants. Afternoon sessions were usually interspersed with other activities such as physical education, television programmes, assemblies and other events. We did not expect any dramatic changes in the children's general literacy levels when they spent so little time using the software, but we did expect to see them develop different ways of writing and learning with the software and hoped for some substantiation of the claims we had constructed.

To determine whether the NIMIS classroom had any effect on literacy development we gathered data from a similar class where the children were on average five months younger than those in the NIMIS class and had a different teacher. But they all had the same curriculum and all three teachers planned their teaching activities together. Over the whole academic year the children's story-writing capacity increased dramatically but this is fairly normal during year one at primary school. The national curriculum assessment levels in writing are extremely crude, based on single examples of creative writing. Some children from each class were absent when the assessments took place, but the evidence does suggest that the NIMIS classroom children remained approximately one NC level above the other class throughout the year. The children in both classrooms improved by approx 1.5 NC levels on average between the December and July assessments.

Standardised reading tests, though still difficult to administer accurately for such young children are more accurate than the NC writing assessments. The children's reading ages changed substantially over the year. Those in the NIMIS classroom began the year nine months above the norm in reading attainment. They should have increased by approximately nine months between the September and July testing, but actually increased 14 months. Unfortunately the children in the other classroom, (a slightly smaller group of 20) were too young to test in September. Though both groups finished the year with reading ages well above the norm, the NIMIS class averaged an extra two months over the other class beyond the age and time difference. This may be tentative evidence, which we were not really expecting (given the small samples and various complications) but it does suggest that the children in the NIMIS classroom had greater support for their literacy development. We are aware however that the classes have different children, different numbers and different teachers. The NIMIS class also revealed a much greater range of attainment in reading than the other class, reading ages varying by 42 months compared with 25 months in the other class in April, when the younger class were first tested. A larger class with a greater attainment range was likely to make greater demands on a teacher in terms of meeting individual differences for the development of reading, so any additional gains might be considered less likely.

July 2000	NIMIS class	Other class
Mean Reading Age in months	93.69	86.45
Mean Chronological Age in months	79.48	74.35
Mean Difference in months	14.22	12.1

Within the average improvement of 14 months there are different stories to tell. The two highest achievers made the smallest gains but the story for them is more complex as the National Curriculum Literacy strategy does not cater as well for such children as it does others. They have a very high reading age anyway and are at the very top of the range for the reading test and the results may be less accurate by the final test. The children who made most gains are mainly those in the middle and lower areas of the attainment range. One child made an improvement of over three years and eight others around two. Four of these were some of the lowest attaining children, but this meant they had had extra literacy support throughout the year.

Some of the children felt able to explain how they thought the NIMIS software helped them to read, even though they didn't spend very much time on it in total. Evidence from the computer logs also shows that they spent considerable amounts of time selecting words and phrases from the word bank and hearing them read using the speech synthesis. We compared stories developed using *T'rrific Tales* with stories developed through normal classroom activities. We make some observations on the writing process, as well as about the product:

- The children collaborate informally face to face around the computer workstations to make suggestions about the story and to offer help with the computer interface.

- The emphasis on collaboration in *T'rrific Tales* is consistent with the process which involves the teacher consulting with the pupils at various stages of the writing process; the children then edit their work with the help of a peer; and finally publish the stories for the class or school to read.

- The provision of the word bank changes the normal writing process in classrooms by providing a list of frequently used words derived from the national curriculum for English language, words to describe the pictures, and suggestions for beginnings, middles and ends of stories.

- The use of an affective software agent (Louisa) also changes the writing process because the children receive support, encouragement and suggestions from a friendly character.

In terms of the written product, the *T'rrific Tales* stories that have been examined have a closer relationship between the pictures and the words than the usual classroom stories. The illustrations in the classroom stories are not closely coupled with the text. There is a typically a lot of text underneath one picture but sometimes only one picture for multiple pages. The stories are mostly text based. The *T'rrific Tales* stories have a stronger coupling between pictures and stories, especially in stories written by the higher ability children who were experienced with the software. These stories resemble cartoons in that the pictures supplement the information given in the text with speech and thought bubbles. Inexperienced users of T'rrific Tales sometimes create a picture and then use the word bank to describe the picture. This is similar to the writing produced by pupils when they are first learning to write: the text describes the picture and there is no plot. As the children grow more confident with the software and learn to use features such as multiple frames, the narrative quality of the product improves.

The children write stories which contain creative mixes of characters from school and fairy tale scenarios where, for example, the queen comes to school or the teacher gets involved with a witch. Creativity and conflict was embedded within the characters themselves with the help of the speech and thought bubbles. In one story a baby was shown thinking how bored it was because it had to watch a love scene between the prince and princess.

These ideas certainly show an increased ability to take a range of different perspectives. There is no obligation to mix characters from different scenes and children can keep the more conventional characters appropriate to their scenes – children in school, kings and queens in the castle. But the authors have gained great enjoyment from mixing and matching their characters. They also enjoy the contrasts, which empower them and let them laugh at the authority figures, e.g. 'Lucy gets special powers' and 'the day the head teacher forgot how to spell'. In one story a teacher sat on the ceiling and in others children and babies were given magic wands. The software is designed to allow the children to envisage more equal empathic relationships than traditional hierarchies. At the final interview one child said:

> 'I like swapping with other people. Like sometimes I might swap the castle to the school and the school to the castle'

The reason was: 'because it's really nice and it makes things different'

Because the software means the picture or story can be changed relatively easily the children tend to draft and redraft more than they normally would. This might appear to be wasting time because it can take longer for stories to be created but there is much thinking, discussion, vocabulary learning and story building going on. The children can play with ideas, change them and redraft them as they work. They also take ideas from the word banks and reform them into new and different ideas. Typing is slow for these 5 and 6 year olds although they are much quicker and more adept at using the computer interfaces than other children of comparable age. Because of the word banks, words are more likely to be found and spelled correctly, which takes longer in terms of finding, but less in terms of typing because they can be dragged into situation. The words are also more readable because of the higher legibility of typewritten words over handwritten, and they are more easily re-read by the children when they present their stories to the class. Handwritten stories may be difficult to remember and re-read because they are scrawled and misspelled. The cartoon stories are clear and short. The children have been able to relate pictures directly to words and to hear any words of which they were unsure. This provides a multi-media way of learning. The fun element in the stories helps to trigger emotions and improves the children's memory, aiding subsequent reading.

Asked what she thought about the about the word banks one child said: 'Err – I love all of them' . She explained how she really felt she was learning when the word banks arrived:

> 'I really felt I could learn a lot and not forget about it, because I do like descriptions, I like that description button a lot because I use it lots of times'.

Another explained:

> '...like in *T'rrific Tales* you just click on the word and if you click the button underneath..well it's a got a sound and you put your headphones on and you can read it, the headphones can help you read it'.

Another child said of the program: 'It's really nice. I really want to play with it every day but I can't' , and, when asked what she liked, said:

> '...writing, drawing, writing stories and putting pictures on-it's really nice. I like playing on...words, playing on pictures of children and teachers, dinner ladies, daddies coming to pick them up, mummies, brothers ... everything.'

These three children cover the attainment range in the class, so clearly the software is engaging them all across the four years reading age. The last respondent also demonstrates how important it was to choose familiar settings as part of the software. No 'daddies and mummies and brothers' were specified in the software but her imagination immediately made the leap from what she saw and she was able to relate it to her own experience. This is why story hearing and writing is so important for children. They can build on what they know and eventually relate it to something beyond their current family, learning about the perspectives of a much wider range of people.

Key Outcomes

The overriding impressions of the NIMIS classroom at Glusburn are of a highly successful project with interesting and detailed findings on the implementation of a Year One classroom of the future. The literacy software proved popular with the children, and the word banks, writing support and speech synthesis facilities were all extensively used to write stories. The project had ambitious goals, as did the other ESE projects. The work has been presented in terms of how the classroom functioned, how well children collaborated, how well the various interfaces for children and teachers operated and how well the software worked in assisting the children to develop important aspects of literacy. We can see interrelationships between, for example, how children collaborated with each other and how their story writing skills were developed.

To summarise the effectiveness of the classroom:

- it was easy to use after the first few weeks of introduction

- it has been highly valued, used and enjoyed by both pupils and teachers all year and across the curriculum

- children have had more opportunities to present and interact in whole class sessions

- children have had more opportunities to collaborate in different ways and by the end of the project they often chose to write stories together

- the children are now confident, and have worked well together. They have time for each other and have built a good philosophy of helping one another

- teachers have found the classroom flexible and supportive of their teaching and would not now want to be without the NIMIS facilities

Since the project ended we have been able to present this work in a variety of contexts. What we have found is that the principles underlying the design of the NIMIS classroom have face validity for school teachers. It is particularly significant that this approach contrasts strongly with the current UK trend to use separate computer laboratories in primary schools. We believe that the principles underlying the design of our classroom are highly relevant and important for the UK. We don't claim that they will automatically work in other educational systems and other cultures but we believe the approach will have widespread application.

The project also supports collaboration:

- children have collaborated in a wide variety of ways

- collaboration is complex and occurs at different levels, as the NIMIS classroom provides a range of experiences through its layout, different hardware and software interfaces

- successful collaboration depends on many factors, not least high quality of interaction, high levels of engagement and the sharing of control in collaborative tasks. This is more likely to occur amongst friends.

- low quality interaction occurs most when an individual dominates the task, but this is inhibited by the NIMIS structure

- children are less engaged when obliged to be passive for long periods but this doesn't happen around the computers

About the interfaces between digital devices and children/teachers that support learning we found that:

- after the first few weeks the hardware proved easy to use by both teachers and children

- the software has been used effectively to create stories showing creativity and reflecting more than one perspective

- children have used the story support within the software to improve their story-writing, helped less by the teacher and more by peers

- children have made good use of the story supports and speech synthesis

- children have successfully worked together to write stories

- the agent generated positive initial reactions

The analysis of gains in the children's literacy is complex, and our conclusions need to be critically examined. What we believe we have shown is that:

- the software even without some possible refinements and different levels, has proved popular and stimulating for the children, who have produced many interesting stories with differing perspectives

- the children have been able to create some quite elaborate stories with minimal teacher support

- their literacy levels have improved beyond the comparative class, and beyond the norm

- the process of writing stories using the software differs markedly from pen and paper writing and encouraged much more drafting and editing

- children were deeply engaged when using the computers and software

Towards the end of the project, it was evident that further development was needed. The user-friendly and interactive nature of *T'rrific Tales*, combined with its flexibility, have meant that we have had considerable interest in it from many sources. Software houses have approached us over its future publication and educationalists have suggest developments and uses of the application beyond its original intention of supporting literacy and narrative development with 5 and 6 year olds. Special needs teachers in secondary schools and teachers of English as an additional language have shown particular interest, as have modern foreign language teachers who can foresee it being used with multilingual word-banks.

Government agencies, teacher trainers, school inspectors, educational advisers and teachers of adult literacy have also shown interest. Thus there are numerous possibilities for exploration, and for research into the forthcoming agent technology, if we can obtain further funding. To some extent the success of the software interfaces is also dependent on the layout and size of the hardware interfaces. Accordingly, we would probably choose larger WACOMs and perhaps fewer children to each table in a future project.

Inevitably many research questions have been generated by the project. Our data collection methods, like many other classroom interventions, suffer somewhat from researcher intervention, so that it is difficult to assess how the classroom would function in more normal contexts. This concern is partly being met through follow up research supported by the Nuffield Foundation – 'Humans and Computers working together in Schools: Improving Achievement, Motivation and Self-esteem with ICT in Key Stage One', or as we call it, 'ICT and the Whole Child'. The methodology requires us to stand further back from the classroom. It also allowed us to design and install a room for a Year Two class in the same school and observe the development of a class of children moving through Year One and Year Two, giving us double the time in to check some of the findings of the NIMIS project.

Though there are many software applications and computer systems which aim to improve achievement, this project is unusual in its whole classroom approach and in combining the assessment of both personal and academic skills. The NIMIS project was the main project in the recent EU funded Experimental School Environments group which considered the whole classroom environment in its evaluation. For us the context in which ICT is used is central to its evaluation. This is becoming increasingly recognised as a key factor in designing successful technological learning environments.

Chapter Three

éTui: scaffolding children's reflection with behaviour based robots

David Griffiths and Josep Blat

Dept. de Tecnologia,
Universitat Pompeu Fabra,
Barcelona, Spain

Introduction

*é*Tui is a robotic toy designed to support meta-level reflection for 4 to 8 year olds The prototype was developed from 1999 to 2001 by a consortium of Ultralab, Universitat Pompeu Fabra (UPF), Apple, and the University of Trondheim[3]. The appearance of the toy was the responsibility of UPF, and we would particularly like to acknowledge the creativity and enthusiasm of Claudia Torres, the designer, as well as the fabrication skills of Margalida Abrams. Ultralab designed the behaviours and hardware: Kris Poppat programmed the 2D presentation, Weiya Wang assembled and programmed the hardware, and Stephen Heppell, Carole Chapman, Andy Simpson and Leonie Lamondt all made contributions. Field trials in England were conducted by Richard Millwood of Ultralab, and Terje Rydland of Trondheim University coordinated the trials in Norway.

When robots have been used in schools in the past, the focus has largely been on the use of construction kits and programming environments. Our work, in contrast, focused on understanding how children respond to computational toys such as the éTui, and how they could be used to facilitate children's ability to reflect. Our results indicate the appropriate characteristics of such a toy, and the potential of this educational approach.

The final prototype consists of a substantially modified *Descartes* robotic kit, covered by a shell. The toy is autonomous, and holds seven programs in memory

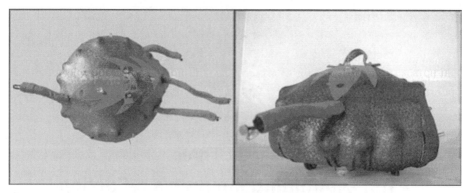

Figure 2: One of the seven working prototypes produced

for the user to select from. There are four paired LED and light sensor assemblies mounted on flexible tubes, enabling the toy to sense the presence of an obstacle. Sensors are also included on the wheels, so that the toy can detect that it has been blocked, and provide input on motion when it has been pushed along. An independent motor running both forward and backwards on each drive wheel, four coloured LEDs, and a sound generator provide output.

The user gives commands to the toy by pressing a switch concealed in the padded shell, which provides seven options corresponding to the notes of the diatonic scale. Some commands can also be given by flashing lights into the sensors. Play activities with the toy involve patterns of interaction between the toy and its environment (wandering, following a path, finding a way out of an enclosure...), including the child's interventions. The appearance and behaviours of éTui were designed in collaboration with children at the three partner schools[4], in activities integrated into the schools day to day activities.

The theoretical context that informed the development of éTui was constructivism. There is no space in this chapter to discuss this in detail, but clearly Piaget and Vygotsky are reference points without which our work is barely conceivable. From the former derives the fundamental insight that children acquire by constructing meaning for themselves from their lived experiences, rather than being provided with facts which they store up, and that they do so according to a pattern of developmental stages. Vygotsky came to believe that 'the central fact about our psychology is the fact of mediation'(Cole and Wertsch, 2002)[5]. In other words, we understand the world through the use of mental or physical tools which are provided by the social environment. He proposed the concept of the Zone of Proximal Development (ZPD) (Vygotsky, 1978 p.86), summarised by Bruner as 'an account of how the more competent assist the young and the less competent to reach that higher ground from which to reflect more abstractly about the nature of things' (Bruner, 1983 p.73). Accordingly, the central role for the successful teacher is to recognise the extent of each individual child's ZPD at a given stage in their development, and to provide mediation and support for them in their learning. Such activity by the teacher provides 'scaffolding', defined as a 'process that enables a child or novice to solve a problem, carry out a task, or achieve a goal that would be beyond his unassisted efforts' (Wood, Bruner *et al*, 1976).

éTui was conceived as a device to assist teachers in providing scaffolding in a particular area, that of reflection by the children on their own cognitive processes, or 'metacognition'. Play with the toy is not intended to create this insight in itself, but rather to offer support for facilitating conversation about the. When discussing robotics use in classrooms for students with special needs, Miller *et al* (2000) speak of scaffolding as 'cautious constructivism'. A number of pedagogic units have been developed to achieve this scaffolding using éTui, and one example of meta-level learning is in the unit *Reflection on Perception*: This uses the wandering behaviour of the robot, which changes to reversing and rotating away from objects in its path. This is used to motivate questions about sensory abilities (sight, hearing, touch), through planned activities such as 'éTui meets a person', or 'showing to a friend', etc. The rich interactions of the children in these activities, and similar situations in the other pedagogic units developed, are analysed later in this chapter.

In developing éTui we found that it was not necessary to create a very intelligent toy with cutting edge robotics and artificial intelligence, but simply one which evokes feelings and impressions of intelligence, interacts with the children, and provokes curiosity and delight. Thus the original contribution of éTui lies in the approach to using robots in education, and the lessons learnt in the design process and trials, rather than in the technological developments which led to the prototype.

Precedents and related work

The approach taken to educational robotics by éTui has been strongly informed by previous work. But there are certain significant contrasts between our work and mainstream developments in the field. An early relevant precedent for éTui is the work of W Grey Walter, who carried out ground breaking research on mobile autonomous robots in the 1940s (Walter, 1950, 1951, 1963). His aim was quite different from our own. He wanted to study the foundation of simple reflex actions, and test the notion that complex behaviour arises from neural interconnections. The robot itself, however, has striking parallels, with its light sensor, touch sensor and its two vacuum tube analogue computer. Despite their simple structure, Walter's robots were capable of intriguing and evocative behaviours, seeking an intermediate light level, moving towards the light, unless it was too intense, in which case they moved away. As its batteries ran down it turned back toward the light in its hutch, backed in, turned itself off, and took 'nourishment' from electrical contacts on the floor (Freeman, 2001).

Some thirty years later Valentino Braitenberg conducted a more focused study of how simple machines can evoke complex emotions in the observer. In his book *Vehicles – Experiments in Synthetic Psychology* (Braitenberg, 1984), he describes fourteen different vehicle designs, and in each one he sets out to generate a different emotion or set or emotions, of increasing complexity. The robots in these thought experiments were driven by two wheels and linked to several sensors. These could detect the intensity of a stimulus, and the control mechanism could vary the speed of the wheels. Braitenberg's vehicles were later implemented with robotic Lego bricks (Hogg, Martin *et al*, 1991) at MIT. In many respects éTui resembles a Braitenberg vehicle, with its two drive wheels, and simple behaviours that generate complex relationships with the environment.

The ability of simple systems to create complex behaviours and give the impression of exploration and emotion is the key for éTui. As Sharkey notes about Braitenberg, 'The inspirational part of the work was in the explanation of how behaviours which we might normally associate with mental activity appear to be created with such limited resources and direct wiring (i.e. running from shadows, or hiding in dark places and pouncing on prey) and even went as far as love' (Sharkey, 1997).

In the 1970s the constructivist perspective on education came together with developments in robotics to generate a fertile new field of research on the use of robots in education. This was exemplified by Seymour Papert's book *Mindstorms – Children, Computers and Powerful Ideas* (Papert, 1980)[6]. Papert proposed that computers could be used as engines which children could teach, and that children would learn by teaching them, thus inverting the traditional relationship. In practice, 'teaching' the computer meant programming it using the Logo language he developed. Children could control a tethered robot, known as a turtle. As the turtle moved around, following the instructions established by the children, it marked its track with a pen, thus allowing the children to observe the consequences of their programming. Papert named his approach *constructionism*, and he stressed that children should be given challenging concrete tasks, and that a positive context for learning should be provided. He described this as 'syntonic learning', i.e. learning which 'is coherent with (the students') sense of themselves as people with intentions, goals, desires, likes, and dislikes' (Papert, 1980, p63). These notions were adopted for éTui.

Resnick and his research group, also working in MIT, believed that children's learning experience could be expanded by supporting them in constructing the robot itself (Resnick, 1993). Construction kits with electronics embedded into plastic blocks were provided which could store instructions downloaded from a computer, and this initiative led to the Lego Mindstorms product.

Resnick later developed a somewhat different approach, which he related to the work of Fiedrich Froebel, who established the first kindergarten in 1837. He describes how 'Froebel's kindergarten was filled with objects for children to play with. Froebel developed a specific set of 20 'gifts'-physical objects such as balls, blocks, and sticks-for children to use in the kindergarten. Froebel carefully designed these gifts to help children recognise and appreciate the common patterns and forms found in nature' (Resnick, Martin *et al*, 1998). Resnick points out that these objects, which he describes as manipulatives, 'generally do not help children learn concepts related to dynamics and systems. Usually, these concepts are taught through more formal methods-involving manipulation of abstract symbols, not physical objects. As a result, these concepts are accessible only to older students, with more mathematical expertise'(Resnick, Martin *et al*, 1998). This insight led to the development of a number of innovative technological learning resources, which he calls 'digital manipulatives'[7]. The éTui may also be considered a 'gift' in Froebel's sense, an object which makes certain aspects of the world more salient.

The idea of teaching a virtual or real robot as a game (see below) has been picked up by commercial toy manufacturers, with Tamagotchi and Furby being particularly successful examples. Much more powerful and probably in a different category is Sony's AIBO, which is conceived in terms of enjoyable activities related to watching the movements of the robot, interacting with it, 'raising' it, controlling it and developing it. (Fujita, Kitano *et, al*, 2000). Robotic toys with a more educational focus include Actimates' Barney which are 'small computers that look like animated plush dolls' (Strommen, 1998, Strommen and Alexander, 1999), and *PETS, a Personal Electronic Teller of Stories* (Montemayor, Druin *et al*, 2000). Barney and PETS seem to have contradictory philosophies. Montemayor states that 'a critical feature of PETS is that the child user is always in control. Unlike products such as the Actimates Barney, where the robot directs the flow of action, and the child follows its instructions, we believe that children should decide their own activity patterns'. But as Strommen says:

> The goal of Barney's design was to use the social mimicry of pretend play, combined with the differential responsiveness of interactive technologies, to provide scaffolded learning experiences for young children, both during toy play and in combination with other learning media.

The éTui robot is a simple device which relates to Brooks' approach to the construction of robots which are situated in their environment, and can interact directly with human beings. He describes this departure from classical artificial intelligence in terms which he designates as situatedness, embodiment, intelligence and emergence (Brooks, 1991). A number of initiatives based on this insight have focused on programming robots by 'teaching' them to imitate human beings, and on interfaces which provide a direct and intuitive interfaces which encourage humans to respond to them emotionally. Brooks *et al* (1998) describe how in the Cog project his team are:

> ...building physical humanoid robots and allowing them to interact with people through behavioural coupling as well as direct physical contact. .... We design these robots to follow the same sorts of developmental paths that humans follow.

Some work with children has been inspired by this approach, for example in the Robota project (Billard, Dautenhahn *et al*, 1998) a doll-like robot is taught to perform different sequences of actions and to label these action sequences with different 'names' through an imitation game, in which the robot mirrors the movements of a 5 year old child's arms and head. In the Aurora project (Dautenhahn, 1999), a pedagogic goal is added to this play activity. The focus is on the contrast between human and robotic forms of interaction, and the aim is to help children with autism make sense of the world. This work is perhaps the closest to ours, although, the autism and metacognition contexts are so wide apart that the apparent differences cannot be discounted.

Scaffolding mediated by éTui

Although linked with the work described above, éTui has a distinct educational approach. With the constructivist tradition, we reject the notion that education consists of a flow of information or knowledge from teacher to learner, and subscribe to the view that education is best understood as a system of conversations of various types, leading to coordination of the behaviours of the actors involved[8]. From this perspective, the educational model derived from Papert's work focuses on a particular kind of conversation, involving a formal language which mediates the conversation, and an apprenticeship model in which learning is recognised when learners are able to produce artefacts which are deemed acceptable by their peers or teachers, or to meet some normative standard. Work has been conducted in this field using programmable Lego bricks (or the more recent 'Crickets'). But the use of an abstract programming language excludes many younger children, who cannot cope with the intellectual challenge it represents and so cannot benefit from the learning resources.

In the traditional kindergarten, objects derived from Froebel's original 'gifts' are very common. These objects are designed to make certain relationships salient. While children playing with these resources may reach an understanding of the relevant concepts on their own, teachers and parents provide scaffolding by regularly intervening, engaging the child in conversation about what they are doing, and introducing new terminology and concepts. We suggest that computational toys, with a much richer behaviour, can be very valuable when used in this way, and that programming may be viewed as simply a highly structured form of interaction, which may be more appropriate when children are older. Young children's interactions with the artefact may be a matter of playing with it, trying to understand its behaviour, and observing that certain patterns of interaction produce certain consequences, providing learning opportunities.

An example of the contrast between these two approaches is the *Curlybot* toy, developed at MIT by Frei *et al* during the period of the éTui project. Its functionality focuses on one of éTui behaviours, the repetition of a movement when the toy is pushed. It can be used for children 'to develop intuitions for advanced mathematical and computational concepts, like differential geometry, through play away from a traditional computer' (Frei, Su *et al*, 2000). In éTui, in contrast, we engaged the children in discussion about memory in relation to this behaviour, asking them if the robot was remembering, and what constituted memory, which is a particular aspect of our general theme of metacognition. Like Grey, Walter and Braitenberg and also supported by Turkle (1984, p.31) in the context of computers, we believe that children's observation of robotic perception and processes invites and stimulates reflection about their own perception and cognition. This is also hinted at in comments in the literature on digital manipulatives, such as Resnick's (1993) account:

> Sometimes, children will shift rapidly between levels of description. Consider, for example, the comments of Sara, a fifth-grader. Sara was considering whether her creature would sound a signal when its touch sensor was pushed: It depends on whether the machine wants to tell... if we want the machine to tell us... if we tell the machine to tell us.

This passage confirms our own experience and provides evidence that computational toys do indeed have great potential as facilitators of discussion about complex matters, such as the issue of causality discussed above. This potential has not yet been fully tapped and with éTui we examine these less explored areas. We believe that the behaviours of a well designed robot, acting in the physical world rather than being limited to the screen, have a still greater potential for eliciting meta-level reflection. There are hints from Papert (Papert and Turkle, 1991, footnote 23) when he describes the Logo turtle as 'body syntonic', a concept which he introduced.

> The Logo turtle was designed to be 'body syntonic,' i.e., to allow users to put themselves in its place. When children learn to program in Logo, they are encouraged to work out their programs by 'playing turtle'. The classic example of this is developing the Logo program for drawing a circle. This is difficult if you search for it by analytical means (you will need to find a different equation), but easy if you put yourself in the turtle's place and pace it out.

This suggests that children find it easier to project themselves into the robotic turtle, and to imitate it, than to interpret an image on the screen. From here it is a natural step to see to what extent the children can imagine the 'world view' of a robot, and to consider the differences between this and their own perception. In *Mindstorms*, Papert comments that he 'began to see how children who had learned how to program a computer could use very concrete computer models to think about thinking and to learn about learning and in doing so, enhance their powers as psychologists and as epistemologists'. (Papert, 1980) p.23. In éTui we sought to achieve a similar overall goal, but through play and experiment with a toy, and through conversation, rather than through abstract programming[9].

The requirement in the UK National Curriculum for young children to be taught meta-reflective skills was an additional practical reason for choosing this area of study and development.

The design of the éTui

Detailed reports on the co-design process[10] used in éTui appear on the project website[11], and the issues are discussed in chapter eight so are not discussed in detail here. First the children in the partner schools brainstormed, producing a wealth of ideas for use in prototype designs and also information about the children's preferences that we could use in interpretating the results of trials. The resulting designs were used in activities with the children, to refine the results and generate new ideas. Four prototype designs were produced: 2D designs, VRML, Maya, and physical prototypes, together with a 2D simulation of the toy's interaction with the environment. In addition to trials of these designs, we also investigated existing computational toys and games with the children in activities integrated into the schools' day to day activities.

Delight and engagement were essential, and we saw that characterisation was a powerful resource to exploit in the educational context. Characterisation could also provide children with an entity with which they can interact, rather than a collection of connected components. Our design trials with children and the subsequent trials of the physical prototype showed, however, that great care must be taken to avoid suggesting that the toy has abilities equivalent to those of, for example, a mammal or a cartoon character.

Children, and to a lesser extent adults, have a strong tendency to anthropomorphise robots (see Braitenberg, 1984) and also simple animals. This seems to be triggered by human beings' instinctive responses to objects moving independently in a space they share. A different illusion is created by design features which, for example, make the robot appear as though it can interact through speech, when it does not understand spoken language. The design of Furby is a case in point – it encourages children to think of it as a pet, with its large eyes, moving eyelashes, large mobile ears and apparent ability to speak.

The initial design approach had been to develop an engaging appearance for the éTui, along the lines of Furby, so that the children would readily engage with the behaviours of the device. But our trials with prototypes and other toys led us to think that the characterisation of éTui should reflect the degree of intelligence and interactivity of the toy. There is an ethical issue here we ascribe to Bertrand Russell's dictum that: 'It should be an absolute principal in all dealings with the young not to tell them edifying lies' (Russell, 1992, p.82). Misleading children as to the capabilities of resources is unacceptable. Secondly, if the children are to reflect on the robot's behaviour, they first have to understand its capabilities and behaviour. This is quite demanding enough for children without complications that have no pedagogic justification. Thirdly, the appearance of the device determines the user's expectations of possible interventions and the results. So if appearance and functionality are unrelated, this may confuse the user. For these reasons we tried to match appearance and functionality in an 'honest' design. We did not set out to mislead the children. This meant that the characterisation had to be handled extremely carefully, the challenge being to exploit the engagement characterisation generates without creating insurmountable difficulties of interpretation. In this respect the story of the design of éTui is about a gradual stripping away of design features, until we were left with a prototype which had the minimal characterisation features required to maintain children's engagement and focus them on the robot as an entity. For example a late decision was taken to remove the eyes from the toy, despite their powerful role in characterisation and engagement, and to replace them with antennae-like structures which drew attention to the sensors, but did not have such strong associations for the children.

In one important aspect, however, trials revealed a significant mismatch: many children wrongly assumed that the toy could detect when it was being picked up. As even the most primitive animals such as worms (which have less perception than the éTui) can detect being picked up, we believe that children assumed that the toy could do so as well. We conclude that either all design references to even simple animals should be removed, or (our preferred option) that the toy should indeed detect being picked up. The behaviours of the éTui were developed in a

2D simulation, used in trials with children and then implemented in the physical prototype, as shown in table 1. We have described the robots as 'autonomous' but the observation made by Beer (1990, p109) is perhaps more pertinent: 'Active exploration is a fundamental characteristic of living organisms. If unthreatened, animals start exploring, which is a means to actively gather information. Controllers for exploratory behaviour ... are a first step towards autonomous behaviour'. Apart from the éTui's tunes related actions (which we have not yet explored educationally), its actions are strikingly similar to Beer's virtual insect: turning (to follow straight lines), wandering, recoil response (for collision avoidance) and edge following (which we did not include).

Action	Description
Wandering insect	The toy moves randomly along a number of pre-defined tracks (e.g. circles, '8' shapes and straight lines) avoiding obstacles. If it detects a moving object in front of it, it reverses away. If this happens three times in quick succession, it turns, escapes to a dark area, and shakes. It soon recovers and starts to wander again.
Towards beacons	The toy moves towards the brightest area in its surrounding, avoiding obstacles during the movement. If the readings of four light sensors are the same, *éTui* performs a 'dance' with sound.
Learn tracks	When the toy is pushed along a track, it records the movement. When the control button is clicked the *éTui* repeats the movement. If it detects an obstacle, it turns to avoid it and then repeats the track.
Learn tunes	The toy can be taught to play tunes. Notes and duration can be entered by flashing a torch aimed at an appropriate light sensor. If the *éTui* has played a tune twice it remembers it. If the newly entered note sequence is already in memory, it plays the remaining notes.
Play tunes	The toy plays pre-stored tunes while 'dancing'. It avoids obstacles and sometimes stops playing, wanders, and then resumes.
Follow line	The left, right and back are configured facing down, and the toy can follow a black line drawn on a white background, while playing tunes. When there is an obstacle in its way, it turns around to find the line and follow it.
Bounded wandering	The same configuration as 'follow line', but the toy avoids the black areas. This restrains the robot's field of movement.

Table 1. éTui's actions

School activities with éTuis

Trials with the final prototype toy were conducted in the three partners schools from October 2000 to January 2001, with the objective of investigating:

- how the design of éTui is received by children in terms of attractiveness, extended engagement and comparable acceptance by both girls and boys

- the level and nature of philosophical reflection and curiosity about learning, autonomy and sensory perception éTui stimulates.

Prior to work with the éTui a number of introductory activities were carried out, with the children talking about learning in a number of different situations. These ranged from free flowing interviews, a focused interview on Pokemon and learning, and the use of computer games as facilitators of children's understanding of learning.

Trials

A total of 39 sessions with children were carried out with the prototype éTuis, and the activities were structured according to three Units of Practice (UoPs). Three of the toy's behaviours were selected for use in UoPs:

UoP 1, Focus on perception – 'Wandering insect' behaviour. The children often blocked its path, with their hands or with obstacles, and their engagement with the toy also led them to construct homes for it. There was much discussion of the nature of the éTui's perception.

UoP 2, Focus on autonomy orientation – 'Bounded wandering behaviour'. A simple maze was used, and the toy moved around the bounded area rather like a fly stuck in a bottle, and eventually found its way out. The children were engaged in discussion about whether it wanted to find its way out, the problems it encountered in doing so, and the way in which they would have approached the situation, had they a similarly limited sensory perception of the world.

UoP 3, Focus on learning – 'Learn tracks' behaviour. The facilitator and children pushed the toy along a path, and the toy then repeated this movement. The children were engaged in discussion of whether the toy was learning when it performed this action, and whether they learnt in the same way.

During the activities the facilitator discussed with the children their opinions about the toy's actions, perception, ability to learn, with the aim of relating these to the children's own capabilities. Some written and graphic responses were also obtained from the children, but the facilitators noted that with children of this age written activities often proved less productive than dialogue. The teacher might decide to use the éTui as a stimulus for written work or ask the children to report on what they have learnt, but facilitated dialogue seemed to be more effective as a means of reflection.

To facilitate careful analysis of the experiences nearly all the sessions were recorded on video, and most of this has been transcribed and incorporated into a database, together with the facilitators' comments. Having a searchable corpus of the work done greatly enhances the usefulness of the data generated in the trials. This database contains around 20,000 words of text, and represents a significant resource for further analysis, and for subsequent research.

Gender

Gender use stereotyping refers to the tendency of children to classify toys as only being appropriate for either boys or girls. It was evident at the outset of our work when we asked the children to draw their ideal imaginary toy. There was a polarisation between the boys and the girls, with the girls showing a strong preference for dolls and other figures which imply a personal relationship, while the boys showed a strong preference for toys which are tools for movement and exploration. The éTui is a robotic toy which explores space, and thus in danger of being stereotyped as appropriate only for boys. We doubt that true gender neutrality is an attainable or measurable goal, and so settled for the pragmatic goal of producing a design which was appealing to girls without alienating boys by resorting to stereotypes of femininity. Despite the clear gender bias displayed in the initial activity of drawing an imaginary toy, there was no discernable difference between the attractiveness of the éTui to the girl dominated group in one school, and the other groups with higher numbers of boys. We conclude that our pragmatic design goal was met by coupling exploration behaviours with the insect-like appearance, inherited from the strong characterisation work we had initially developed.

Children also attribute gender to the toys they play with. It is neither possible nor desirable to discourage this. The design team, however, made every effort to avoid gender explicitness so the children could be free in their attribution. Most children were able to say whether they thought the éTui was male or female, and some grasped the slightest indicator as a clue to the toy's gender. For example Auba[12] in Majorca described a pair of éTuis as follows:

> AUBA: This one's brave.
>
> FACILITATOR: Why do you say that it's brave?
>
> AUBA: Because this one's the man and that one's the woman. (later she identified a female éTui: 'Because women have more hair, and it hardly falls out at all')

In another session, however, another girl attributed male gender to the same éTui on the basis of its white fur. Thus it seems inevitable that gender attributions will be made by children in terms of their pre-existing world view. It is, however, a positive indicator of acceptance that a number of girls identified the toy as female.

Children have a strong tendency to project animate intelligence onto the toy; an intentional interpretation

The toy provides the children with relatively few cues for anthropomorphic projection, but despite this they sometimes speak to the toy as if it were human, or a pet. They typically greatly overestimate the intelligence of the toy, and then gradually arrive at a more realistic evaluation as they observe its behaviour. For example, on his first contact with the toy, Gabriel said:

> Facilitator: So, how come it doesn't bang itself?
>
> Gabriel: It's very clever.
>
> Facilitator: Why is it clever? Do you think...
>
> Gabriel: Because when it touches something it goes somewhere else. It's very clever.

Similarly in the previous day's trial, Auba attributed feelings to the toy:

> Auba: No, no, It's naughty. Careful. It doesn't want to. 'Hello, helloo'. No, leave it alone.
>
> Facilitator: Do you like doing that to it?
>
> Auba: No, because it's saying 'Don't do that to me'.
>
> Facilitator: Why do you think that it wants to get out?
>
> Auba: Because it probably hasn't got enough space

The attitudes of the children to the toy varied. Some, such as Auba, kept ascribing greater awareness and emotion to the toy than did other children. Although she was not upset when the toy was stuck or trembling, she did seem to be concerned for it. Her classmate, Francisca, on the other hand, was blasé, and on one occasion damaged the toy by accidentally dropping it on the floor. The children consistently ascribed greater perception to the éTui than it has. While they could understand that the toy perceived the world through its sensors, they had difficulty in understanding it could only respond to inputs in real time from objects in its immediate environment and had no memory or perception whatsoever of anything else. For example a behaviour had been programmed into the toy so that if its path was blocked three times in rapid succession it would shake as if afraid. The idea here was that three blockages would mean that it was being pursued. But the children assumed that éTui could tell someone was coming towards it when it bumped into an obstacle, and so did not see the connection between the three blockages and pursuit[13]. They gave other explanations such as 'it's frightened because we've grabbed its antenna', or said it was because it was dizzy, confused, or even cold. In Dennett's terms[14] the children were taking the intentional stance towards the toy, making little attempt to engage with it as a designed system, even though they knew that the project team had been designing the toy with their help for months past. This is an important finding, as so much work with robots in schools focuses on the design stance in explaining functionality. It suggests that with younger children, such as those involved in éTui, approaches in which the children take the intentional stance may be more appropriate, and the activities defined in the éTui UoPs provide examples of how this can be achieved. Our experience as facilitators also shows how hard it is for designers, who are naturally working from the design stance, to understand the view of a child to whom this stance is inaccessible[15]. This is important to take into consideration when designing educational applications of robotics, and it is a powerful argument in favour of co-design methodologies.

The children's attempts to understand the gulf between their projections and the toy's actual performance provide the basis for problem solving activities with rich learning opportunities[16]. They were keen to be engaged in reflection about the nature of the toy and its capabilities, and even talked about this spontaneously. But facilitation was needed to guide their reflection. The role of the facilitator is to provide appropriate activities with the toy, to structure these activities for the children, and to intervene so as to make the implicit questions explicit. In the first UoP, for example, the focus is on the éTui as exemplifying a certain type of perception. While playing with the toy the children can observe regularities in its behaviour, and propose explanations, interpretations and creative responses. The facilitator drew attention to key aspects of the toy's behaviour, such how it avoided obstacles, and asked questions about its 'vision'. The children's responses varied. Some believed that it could see 'a bit like us' and recognise its friends by looking at them. Others thought it could only see the world in a cloudy way. The issue for us was not the accuracy of their opinions, but rather that the éTui could stimulate such discussions. In this sense the éTui is an extension of teachers' traditional practice of providing the children with first hand experiences as a support for understanding abstract concepts, rather like using a set of measuring cans and a bucket of water to explore volume, or paper cut outs to explain the concept of area. The 'honest design' principal was crucial. With the éTui prototype one girl, for example, mistook the power socket for an 'eye', and failed to notice a sensor at the back of the toy, presumably because she expected 'eyes' to be at the front. It is easy to imagine how much more confusing it would have been if the toy had been given a recognisable face.

While the children understood the limitations of the éTui's perception well enough to compare it with their own, they did not understand how it worked. As the éTui moved around, it flashed lights for the sensors to detect reflections, and made beeps each time an obstacle was detected. These lights and sounds delighted the children but they did not perceive their role in the toy's navigation. For example, they interpreted the beeps as a kind of communication rather than as feedback from the interface:

> Girl 1: It's made a noise.
>
> Facilitator: And what does this noise mean?
>
> Girl 2: That it's shouting something to its friend.
>
> Boy 1: It's like an alarm, that it doesn't know how to get by.

It is difficult to know whether this misconception indicates the need to use less abstract markers for events such as 'obstacle detected' to allow young children to make the connection, whether they just need longer interactions with it, or whether the behaviour is inappropriate for an 'insect' of this type.

Meta-level reflection can be achieved using the éTui, but it takes time

Young children do not find meta level discussion easy. Our work with computer games, and other interviews, showed that reflection about their own perception and learning is hard for most children of this age. The interviews with children about their own leaning showed that most found this difficult to discuss in the abstract. Even when given a more concrete focus, such as learning the skills to play a new game, they still found it difficult to discuss their own cognitive processes. In our pedagogy, meta-level reflection builds on their reflection on the nature of the toy. When children have formed a view of the toy which may or may not be scientifically correct but which provides them with a satisfactory explanation for their observations, they can move on to discussing the differences between their own capabilities and behaviour and the behaviour of the toy. These processes take time, and it is unsurprising that the most interesting reflections generally occurred after several sessions with the toy. For example in their third session, after relatively superficial interactions, this was their response:

> Facilitator: Do you think that this creature has got a map like that? (referring to the toy)
>
> Marc: No. All this looks new to him (indicates the bounded area)

Facilitator: And when it explores, is it making a map in its head?

Marc: Yes

The children then compared the performance of the toy with their own experience of the world and the way they orient themselves:

Facilitator: So, is that how you do it, or is it different for you?

Natàlia: Yes

Lourdes: No, no it isn't different, no

Facilitator: No it isn't different

Natàlia: For me it is

Facilitator: So how is it?

Natàlia: It's like, how much distance I've done. (i.e. she was using dead reckoning)

Finally agreement was reached that the toy could not make a map in its head, but that the children could. Though appropriate to the 7 or 8 year olds, the discussions dealt with the complex issue of whether their own navigation skills were based on cognitive maps or a step by step process.

The children's response to the toy went through phases

While the structure of UoPs developed for use with the éTui divided activities into three themes, it was noted that the children responded to the toy in a three phase pattern which cut across this division:

1. initial enchantment and a tendency to project intelligence and animate qualities onto the toy. This response occurs when there is no adult intervention.

2. a problem solving stage, where the behaviour of the unknown artefact challenges the children to describe and understand it. Children sometimes engage in such problem solving activity in the course of their play with the toy, but a facilitator can greatly help their reflection.

3. an opportunity for reflection on the differences between the toy's ability and their own. Children seldom enter this stage spontaneously.

We hypothesise that this three stage pattern will emerge in any similar use of interactive toys.

Summary and conclusions

Our work has defined an area of use for robotic and other computational toys, to scaffold reflection by young children. The prototype toy produced by the project has demonstrated that this approach can be successful in the classroom, when supported by an appropriate pedagogic framework. More specifically we observe that:

- children's use of the toy falls into a three stage pattern: fascination, problem solving and reflection. We hypothesise that this is a generalisable pattern of approach to robotic toys
- in this three stage pattern, fascination is spontaneous. Problem solving may be spontaneous but is best supported with facilitation, and reflection usually requires facilitation
- to stimulate reflection a high level of robotic intelligence is not required, although greater sophistication may bring benefits
- children find reflecting on their own cognition hard but not impossible. The éTui (or similar devices) can provide scaffolding for such reflection
- a pedagogic framework focusing on specific areas for reflection helps to draw out children's learning with the toy
- 'honest' design supports the children in their understanding
- the design stance taken by the design team was not shared by the children working on the project. Frequent contact with the user group is therefore essential

The éTui project has demonstrated that the concept it proposes is valid. It has also indicated some design principles for devices that use this approach. The design space of possible robotic devices for supporting young children's reflection is immense, and increases as more sophisticated technologies become available. This space needs to be explored so that the possibilities and limits of the application of robotics as defined by the éTui project can be mapped out. Regularities in the response of children to different types of artefacts can then be analysed, moving towards hypotheses with predictive power which can guide future design. Nevertheless, we continue to examine the breadth of material we have collected, to enhance and develop our understanding. The next practical step is to develop more toys of a similar type, so as to answer the questions that have arisen so far:

- which areas of the subject curriculum can be effectively supported by using similar techniques?
- which behaviours and designs best support children's reflection in relation to these curriculum areas?
- how can more sophisticated artificial intelligence add to the effectiveness of éTui? Technologies which suggest themselves include voice recognition and training, musical interaction, and visual pattern recognition.

- how can a greater degree of situatedness support children's reflection? We have already noted that the éTui should know when it has been picked up, but providing a persistent memory would give it a higher level of sophistication so the child could build up a relationship with the toy. These would be valuable areas to explore, as would the ability to recognise individual users. At present when two éTuis meet they do not distinguish each other from the surrounding environment, but the potential for reflection on communicative behaviour between two toys is well worth exploring.

Looking back on our work in éTui, we believe that we have engaged with an innovative and fascinating line of research, and shown that there is still much valuable work to be done. We hope to continue our exploration in greater depth along the lines we describe here, both with our present partners and the wider research community.

Chapter Four

Making rules in collaborative game design[17]

Celia Hoyles and Richard Noss
Institute of Education
University of London

In early childhood, play and learning are closely connected. In play, the normal constraints of the world, and the ordinary uses of objects, may be suspended to create a stage and props for the working out of inner realities and personal models of the world. According to Piaget, the young child plays in order to disassociate from the immediate and concrete; it frees her to engage in behaviours – particularly fantasies – which would otherwise be too demanding (Piaget, 1951). This imaginative transformation of the world is essential to play, and to its power to support thinking and learning. For this reason – if for no other – the use of games as a learning device can be justified by the possibility of presenting the complexity of diverse situations in such a way that people can test hypotheses and see the results of their decisions.

Sylva (1976) has demonstrated convincingly how this works in practice. Her studies showed that children who were given time to play with objects were better able to solve problems with them than children who had been instructed or given demonstrations. Intriguingly, children who performed best on her problem tasks were those who had included imaginative transformations of the objects in their exploration, such as arranging them to make familiar objects.

In Piaget's view (1932), the development of play progresses from a purely individual process and private symbolism to social play and collective symbolism. Crucially, there are *rules* underpinning play and these are classified into two types: those handed down from above and those constructed spontaneously. It is, according to Piaget, by distinguishing between these two kinds of rules that children learn that rules are not sacred and untouchable but can be modified and adapted. Piaget concluded (largely through an analysis of boys playing marbles), that between ages 7 and 10 years, children were unable to codify rules, although they could play games according to social conventions. A conscious realisation of the rules of their games and seeing that they could be changed, Piaget argued, only developed at age 11-12. For Piaget what changes over time is the explicit recognition of the rules of a game. To sum up the Piagetian view, play helps transform the child's thinking from the concrete to the abstract, and proceeds from the individual to the social.

Vygotsky (1978) elaborates Piaget's perspective in two main ways. First, while Piaget tends to convey the impression that the child is in the position of creating her conceptual world on her own individual account, Vygotsky stresses that the child needs to appropriate the conceptual resources of her culture, effectively reversing the direction of developmental flow from social to individual. Second, Vygotsky argues that play always consists of two interrelated components: an imagination situation, and rules governing the interactions within the imagination. What changes over time is the *explicitness of the rules*. In early pretence play, the overt imaginary situation is governed by a *covert* set of rules: children begin to learn that individual satisfaction can be enhanced by cooperation in rule-governed activities. At the opposite pole, there are games in which the imaginary situation is *covert* and the rules *overt*. For Vygotsky, the long term development of the child is from pretence play to games with rules, and from games with covert to overt rules. Despite the differences between the two theories, there are some important commonalities. In both theories, the development of play is described in a unidirectional manner and pretend play is thought to precede and be largely replaced by games with rules. And in both theories, play has a role in the separation of perception, action and thought, positioned as a transitional stage between contextualised actions and decontextualised thought. Play serves to separate the child from context, and helps to connect informal knowledge with the world of the abstract.

The traditional view, then, is that play matures into games: young children play; older children (and adults) play games[18]. What changes is the rules, and how they are interpreted by the player. But the reality is not so clear-cut: even in rule-bound games, there is spontaneity (Lieberman, 1977). There is an interesting dialectic. Play demands familiarity, the rituals that derive from fluency emanating from the habitual and recognised. Yet genuine creativity necessitates stepping outside the strictly familiar into the relative unknown, voyaging beyond what is already understood into uncharted waters. It is this dialectic between known and unknown, familiar and novel, that provides a motor for creativity (and incidentally, goes some way to explaining why it is that creative discoveries are so often the result of playful and 'off-task' activities).

Digital technologies offer new possibilities for play, affording opportunities for fantasy, challenge, collaboration and competition. But their relationship with learning remains tenuous, and most current computer games typically cast children in the role of game-player, playing according to rules programmed by someone else – a situation which, however motivating, sets strong boundaries around what might be learned, as well as powerful constraints on their appeal.

Without doubt, computer games hold the potential to support many forms of play (e.g. construction or competitive games, games of chance, games of pretence or imitation) and as such have the potential to provide a forum for children to rehearse aspects of the wider social culture. Yet studies investigating the relationship between play and learning in the context of computer games are presently relatively few and far between – perhaps surprisingly so given the tremendous attraction of these games to many children (see Papert, 1998; Rubin, 1995), for thoughtful discussions of these and related issues). The few studies that have addressed this area have focused on the use of electronic games to enhance learning of particular curriculum areas, especially mathematics, Saxe and Bermudez (1992); Steffe and Weigel (1994); Klawe and Philips' EGEMS (1995) or more general cognitive competences, such as problem solving (Nicolopoulou and Cole, 1993).

While it is easy to dismiss computer games' potential for learning, we cannot dismiss the engagement which they engender. Engagement is not the same as learning, but its insufficiency should not blind us to its necessity. As Lara Croft races across the screen, the child controlling her is rapt, engaged to the core, part of the action in every sense. In one sense, of course, Lara is controlling the child – watching kids (and adults) playing games like *Tomb Raider* is a fascinating essay on the mutual engagement of subject and object ... just who is controlling whom? Lara becomes real: the packages advertise her as *starring* in the game. And this engagement with the action of the game, together with the unpredictability of what *she* will do next (there are strict rules which govern what she can and cannot do at any time) is what seems to hold the attention. What she will actually do is not determined until the player is completely expert – at which point, many will disengage, the challenge exhausted.

It is hard to see much to do with learning in this scenario, much less the kinds of learning valued by the culture of school. Posed as a dichotomy between ritualised play on the one hand and creative endeavour on the other, the dichotomy appears extreme. One solution favoured by some educators is to seek to obscure learning behind a clutter of gamelike interaction, as if by wrapping up learning as if it were the same as play, the fundamental need for struggle, for creating mental structures to build understandings, could be suspended. We seek an alternative.

Our challenge has been to design systems and activity structures where learning is the outcome of a synergy of creativity *interconnected* with ritualised play. Rather than see these two forms of interactions as opposite poles, we seek to design systems that build on the relationship between them, exploiting the potential of the former for laying the basis of the latter. A helpful starting point is to notice that when playing games, children necessarily follow the rules of the game designers – the rules are passed down from above. We do not know what the contingencies are that lead players to reflect consciously on the rules governing their play. We know, for example, from our own research into children's interactions in computer microworlds, that there are a range of strategies which can promote reflection: requiring discussion, predicting and explanation in and across multiple forms of expression, organising cognitive and socio-cognitive conflict and encouraging its resolution, supporting debugging and the exploitation of feedback (see for example Hoyles, Healy and Pozzi, 1992; Healy, Pozzi and Hoyles, 1995). What we do not know is how far these strategies can be incorporated into game-playing without destroying the game.

There are some recent attempts to exploit children's engagement at the surface while there are deeper issues underpinning design and therefore learning. Some promising developments have been made where children have been placed in the role of designers. Harel (1998) argued that children gained a deeper understanding of fractions through creating and manipulating fraction representations for the purpose of creating instructional software for other children. Following Harel's work and relating more specifically to games, Kafai (1995) designed computer games for learning together with children. He claimed that designing games for others allowed learning to become instrumental towards intellectual and social goals beyond those of the game itself.

In designing computer games children have the opportunity not only to create, modify and adapt rules – to structure the forms of co-operation and competition, to decide what is a fair result, to begin to appreciate causality and even conditionality – but they do so in the context of a formal system. Can digital games be exploited to help children recognise how rules frame their play? Can we build systems which possess the immediacy of the computer game, the richness of interface design with these deeper goals for learning? Can we get behind the interface without destroying what makes it work? These are all general questions: At a more specific level, in this chapter we begin to address two questions: What are the types of rules that children engage with when they are involved in game building and game playing? And what are the transformation processes that occur during children's experience of different rule types during game playing and game modification at a distance? But first we introduce the design criteria developed as part of the Playground Project.

The Playground Project: some design issues

In the Playground Project (www.ioe.ac.uk/playground), our overriding design criterion was to build a computational environment[19] in which children could build, modify and share games using the formalisation of rules as creative tools in the constructive process. We called these environments 'Playgrounds'. The project aimed to place children in the role of producers as well as consumers of games, and in so doing changed their relationship with the rules, since rules were necessarily raised to a more overt plane, they became objects of reflection, something else with which to play creatively.

We worked with children aged 6 to 8 in various European cities in settings that varied with the educational culture of the country. In London, we worked in an informal out-of-class setting of an inner-city primary school. In preliminary interviews, we asked the children to describe their favourite games (both on and off the computer) and the rules of these games. Not unexpectedly, we found that initially, most only described constraints ('you mustn't hit other children') and not the actual rules designed into the game or the structural constraints that underpinned them ('you have to pick up this object in order to get through that door'). One finding of the project was that this preference became less pronounced as the children developed familiarity with the playground systems and used them to design and build their own games.

The playground system under discussion here was built in *ToonTalk* (Kahn, 1996), a Turing-equivalent parallel constraint-based programming environment, in which animations are the source code of the language; that is, programs are created by directly manipulating animated characters, and programming is *by example* (see Cypher, 1993). In *ToonTalk*, the user can construct programming code by training an animated robot who is given an example input to work on and is shown what to do by the user. Robots are initially constrained to work only when given identical inputs, but their conditions can subsequently be relaxed and generalised, providing for a wider range of operating contexts. *ToonTalk* is object-oriented and a trained robot along with its input box can be attached to the back of an object to give it functionality.

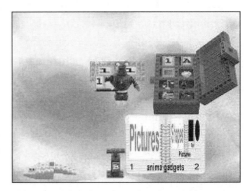

It is not easy to convey the feel of programming with *ToonTalk*: a tiny attempt is given in Figures 3 and 4, in which a robot is trained (i.e. a pro-

Figure 3: A robot is trained to add one value to another

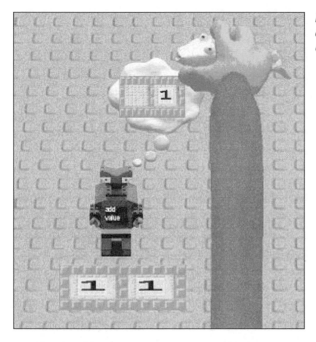

Figure 4: Relaxing constraints by removing details

gram is written) that adds one to a number (in Figure 3, the robot is taught to add 1 to the number 1; and in Figure 4, this constraint that the initial number is 1 is removed). However basic, the example illustrates the sense of formal yet direct manipulation that comprises the programming activity. For more details concerning the principles of Toontalk, together with its rationale and examples, see www.toontalk.com.

We cannot describe any further details of the *Toontalk* platform here, but will dwell on one particular feature of the environment concerning communication between objects and people, since this was exploited in our collaborative game design workshops. Like any object-oriented language, *ToonTalk* needs to provide a mechanism for message passing between objects; and, in keeping with the metaphorical basis of its design, *Toontalk* instantiates this idea with that of a bird flying to its nest. If a bird in *ToonTalk* is given any (reasonable) object, it will deliver this to its nest and then return to its original location. An important development during the project was to extend this metaphor so that a bird could 'fly' to its nest, not only on the same computer but also placed on any other computer on the Internet running ToonTalk. These 'long distance birds' were used so children in different sites could send messages to each other and swap games (see Figures 5a, 5b).

The sight of a bird carrying off (or returning with) an object or message (an object in the form of a text pad, as illustrated in Figures 5a/b) was compelling for

Figure 5a: A message is given to a bird...
Figure 5b: she delivers it and returns to her original position

the children. From our point of view, we intended that they should (and could) see this as a simple extension of the message-passing device between objects with which they had become familiar: certainly all the children we worked with produced viable stories about where the bird was going, how it got there, and why it brought things back. Whether its integration into a coherent computational story was important for this, we simply do not know. Other design criteria were based on the fundamental notion that it must be possible for games and other components within the Playground:

- to afford inspection: where ever possible components could be opened up so that their mechanisms were made more-or-less directly visible
- to entail a common grammar to foster collaborative game-building and game evaluation
- to lend themselves (in the eyes of children) to development and modification.

In order to achieve these criteria, we built a layer of *behaviours*, on top of the *ToonTalk* platform, incorporating elements that allowed young children to gather together functional parts of programming code more easily. In fact, our approach attempted to resolve one of the great challenges that has faced advocates of student programming (see, for example, Noss and Hoyles, 1996) namely, to find just the right grain size of entry into the programming endeavour, which allows something useful to be achieved with minimum intervention into the system, but one which simultaneously invites such intervention. Behaviours are ready-made pieces of programming code that could be re-used, inspected or combined. Thus our aim was that behaviours were visible and functional; both what they did and how they did it were readily available. We also decided that behaviours should be modular, in that each one should be a self-contained piece of code that could be run separately or combined with other behaviours; and they should be interoperable, that is they could easily be transferred between objects while retaining their functionality in the new context.

To be more specific, in *ToonTalk* an object gains functionality by having 'robots on its flipside'. A behaviour comprised these robots along with multi-modal representations of their functionality, that is, text which spoke when pointed at it,

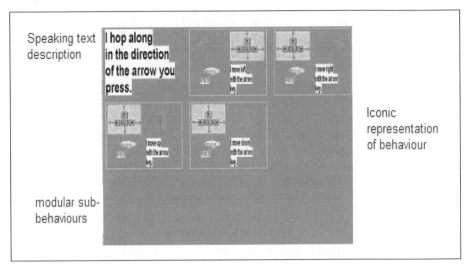

Figure 6: The multi-modal representations of the functionality of behaviours

together with graphical (mostly animated) descriptions. Figure 6 shows the flip side of an object with four behaviours on it. Each one moves the object either right, left up or down and, if packaged as shown together, they will move the object with the arrows. Each individual behaviour can be taken off to disable that functionality component (stop the object moving up, for example) or give it to another object; and each can be changed by editing the robots. We also tried to make the behaviours more shareable by creating conventions in the Playground community – a common grammar in design and labelling – so that children would find it easier to express and share their game designs.

During the Playground project, we watched children build and share games in the different project sites. From analysis of our observations, we elaborated three levels of game modification:

- at the *game* level: changing the aesthetics, where the underlying workings are not touched, but surface features such as colour, sounds etc. are modified[20]
- at the *behaviour* level: swapping, adding or taking away behaviours or doing simple edits of behaviours (e.g. changing values in the input boxes of robots)
- at the *language* (or robot) level: training robots or doing more complex editing of robots

We also noted that when children built their games together on one site (that is face-to face) they adopted two main categories of rules:

The player character

Wizard who sets the goal

A portal that takes the character to the next scene

Figure 7. The first scene in the adventure game

Player rules – regulations that were agreed (possibly tacitly) among the players that should not be transgressed in the interests of the narrative of the game. But there was nothing in the game that 'forced' compliance;

System rules – programmed rules that specified the formal conditions and actions for the objects of the game and their relationships

Coming up with both sets of rules were part of the children's creative endeavour, in order to make a game interesting, maybe challenging, but also, in the Playground context, 'easy to change' by others.

Our focus in the case study presented in part here is on the transformation processes that occurred between player and system rules during collaborative game playing and construction at a distance.

The hunt-the-treasure game

Hunt-the-treasure was an adventure game built by the researchers, rather than by children (again, this decision was based on an attempt to resolve the 'grain size' problem referred to above), where all the objects in the game had on their flip side simple modular behaviours. The initial game consisted of what we call a (player) character controlled by the game player, navigating through several scenes with the goal of finding a treasure (the first scene is shown in Figure 7). Along the way there are obstacles to be avoided and additional 'powers' to be picked up. Each scene contains one or more portals, which could be visible or hidden. When the character touched a portal, she (the user could choose the gender) was transported to a new scene.

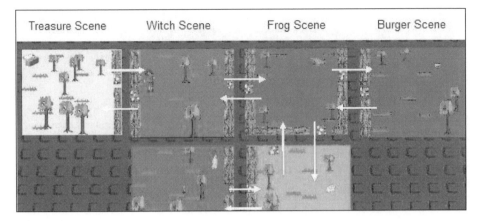

Figure 8. Schematic of the hunt-the-treasure game

The game originally comprised six scenes (see Figure 8 for a schematic of the game). In the first scene, there is a wizard who delivers a message when touched by the character, telling her about the treasure in the forest. Initially, the character can only move horizontally but, by moving into the second scene and 'eating' some cheese (see Figure 8), she gains the power to move vertically. By passing through the third scene and avoiding the bouncing frog (which will 'destroy' the character if touched), the character reaches the burger scene. Upon 'eating' the burger, she gains another new power, to 'shoot' white balls. These can be used to 'kill' the frog and, in the subsequent scene, the witch who 'guards' the portal to the last scene, where the treasure can be found. A triumphant sound is played when the treasure is 'won' by the character.

We have described the game in terms of its narrative. A crucial facet of game-building that children had to learn, was how to translate the virtual phenomena that we put in inverted commas into programmable actions (for example 'eating' in the narrative above). Unsurprisingly, we found that there was nothing natural in this. Some children came up with behaviours that would have the desired effects but clearly had little idea how to build them. By the end of the project however most children were able to harness their imagination so that they were able to codify the rules, but some continued to have difficulty. For example, we noted that even late in the project, some children still wove immensely complex scenarios they would like to program, although they were quite out of reach of their expertise or even the programming system! Returning to the *hunt-the-treasure game*, the changes that children could and did make were as follows: adding a new scene (which meant adding a portal to and from it) or altering the sequence of scenes; changing the appearance of scenes; modifying interactions between objects on any scene; adding and changing objects and their behaviours;

changing the goal of the game; adding and changing communicative aspects of the game by labelling objects and behaviours using text labels (that could speak) or *help* characters that could speak pre-written advice.

Building games collaboratively

Alongside Playground's concerns for game building by children was our desire to create an international community of child game designers, players and evaluators. To achieve these aims, we staged several one-day workshops where children in different countries shared, played, changed and evaluated each other's games synchronously in an online community using a mixture of web-based and in-house technologies. There follows an account of episodes that illustrate some of the issues that emerged.

Two groups of children – in London and in Stockholm – took part in the work-shop, the children in each site teamed up with partners in the other site. Internet video conferencing was set up to facilitate the organisation of the workshop and also to give the children a 'sense of presence' of their partners. This turned out to have an extremely important effect on the running and experience of the work-shop. Dialogue was in English with a researcher/interpreter in Sweden, but never-theless, most of the children cited the video conferencing to talk to their partners as the most enjoyable aspect of the workshop. Long distance birds were used to send and receive games, evaluations and to communicate ideas for game im-provements.

Prior to the workshop, the London children spent four one-hour sessions familiarising themselves with *hunt-the-treasure* through a series of activities, designed to provide them simultaneously with insights into the workings of the game and us with insights into their conceptualisations of how the game worked. With a researcher playing a supporting role they then designed and implemented changes to the game. Their activities were driven by the children's ideas and needs. In early sessions, new scenes for the game were designed on paper and the different rules that would be incorporated into the game were discussed. The sessions were audiotaped and – where appropriate – videotaped; these data were supplemented by logs of the child/computer interactions.

EPISODE 1: Translations from narrative to player rules: creating a new scene

Sarah and Jane, both aged eight, had been programming and creating games in Playground for about a year. They began by discussing a new scene to add to *hunt-the-treasure*, and the role they wanted each of the objects to have in it. At this point, their discussion was characterised by the fictional or narrative account of the way they wanted their scene to work, although we discerned some traces of their anticipation of what could be done in the Playground, that is the ways that the medium shaped their discourse (we should not underestimate the extent to which experience of playing and understanding the mechanisms of the games framed the discourse and even the imagination of the children: we do not discuss here the extent to which this shaping is desirable from a pedagogic point of view[21]). We focus on their description of the 'aliens' they wanted in the scene, whose role would be to 'guard' a bottle of oxygen.

> Sarah: There's an astronaut he's trying to get out of space and he's running out of oxygen. There's going to be a bottle of oxygen but the aliens are guarding it they don't want him to get any. ...If he (the player character) gets some oxygen, he passes the level since the oxygen is like an entrance ... (the children call a portal an entrance).

Sarah's plan was that in the new scene, the player character would have to avoid the aliens to get to the oxygen, which would serve as a portal to another scene. What the children actually did was somewhat different, and shaped by their prior programming experience. The researcher had a crucial role in helping the children to translate their narrative plans into a series of behaviours. For example, to construct an oxygen bottle as a portal, it was suggested that they could obtain the functionality they wanted by copying one of the portals from the existing game, after which they could make it look as they wanted it to by placing the behaviours on the back of a picture of an oxygen bottle. Jane takes up this suggestion:

> Jane: We'll take the behaviours off it (the existing portal)

Jane knew that how the portal looks is unimportant. What makes it do the right thing are the behaviours on its back: a significant insight. The children continued to build and discuss aspects of their scene. They wanted to add some aliens to the scene to 'guard' the oxygen. At the moment the children are referring to a 'real world' interpretation of 'guarding'. What could this mean in the programmed environment? Eventually, and after prolonged discussion, they agreed that one alien would move around in a circle around the bottle, which would constitute 'guarding' the oxygen, and added a behaviour to do this. The interpretation of this movement as guarding was a *player rule* agreed only between the two English girls. At this point, the researcher asked them about it:

> Int: Is this a good or bad alien?
>
> Sarah: They're all bad
>
> Int: What do you want the aliens to do?
>
> Sarah: They're trying to guard it
>
> Int: How do they guard it?

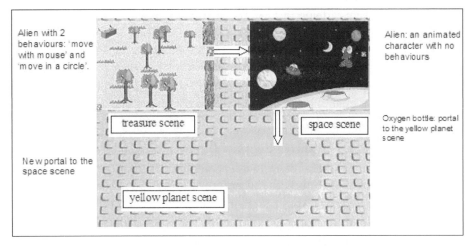

Figure 9. The three final scenes of Sarah's and Jane's space game

> Sarah: This alien is flying all around and he is going to be above the oxygen bouncing and then there are going to be more aliens all around...

The second alien was simply animated and this animation was again a player rule that was agreed to mean guarding. The children completed their space scene by adding the two aliens and oxygen bottle with all their behaviours to an appropriate space scene background – one of the many objects and programs available in Playground. They then had to decide where the player character would go to after moving 'through' the oxygen bottle. They added a new scene, which they called the 'yellow planet'. This scene consisted of a yellow oval, with no further objects or functionality. The idea that it was a planet was somehow generalised from their previous space scene. Their last step was to connect this latest scene to the rest of the game by adding an extra portal to the treasure scene. Their final adventure game was called 'The space game'. Figure 9 shows the changes made and the final sequence of three scenes in the game shared with their partner pair in Sweden.

Sharing the game but not the rules

At the start of the workshop, Sarah and Jane sent their game to Jacob and Ricard, their Swedish partner pair, who at once played the game. They focused on trying to discover any new features or scenes that had been added to the original version of the game. After they had played it a few times, a researcher in Sweden asked them what they liked about the changes and how they thought the game could be extended still further. The boys remarked:

> Jacob: The space scene had some space things and a guy you could control

Int: Ricard, what did you think of the changes?

Ricard: Good, very good (in English)

Int: Jacob?

Jacob: Yes, good but the last scene it (referring to the yellow planet scene) one has to be able to do things there. Else it's no fun discovering

From their play and the interview, it was clear that Jacob and Ricard liked the changes made by their friends in England. However, they had little idea that the 'space things' were supposed to be guarding anything, so could not really connect the new space scene with the general narrative of the game (i.e. getting to the treasure). The player rules were not clear to the children at a different site, who could not interpret the meaning of the behaviours in narrative terms. They were also obviously disappointed that nothing happened in the yellow planet scene, and communicated their feelings through messages with long distance birds. (They were unable to discuss the game effectively over the net because of language difficulties, so their London partners were not provoked to help them understand the purpose of the 'space things' or to add some behaviours to the yellow planet). However, in the second episode below, we see how a closer collaboration did help transform unspoken player rules into system rules.

EPISODE 2: Adding a scene with no game narrative

Helen and Rachel started planning a tropical island scene, called Dragon Island, to add to *hunt-the-treasure*. It would have palm trees and pre-animated pictures as decorations on a background of a yellow oval. Despite suggestions by the researchers, they resisted using behaviours to enhance their scene or to fit it into the narrative of the game or even make it more like a game. The girls were satisfied with their tree plus three animated animals, a bouncing dragon, a blinking panda bear and a fluttering butterfly (see Figure 10). In addition to focusing on decoration at the expense of increasing functionality, they failed to see that they needed a portal to leave the Dragon Island and reach another part of the game (although after prompting, they did link it into the rest of the game so at least you could get into to it!). There was, however, no apparent narrative connecting Dragon Island to the rest of *hunt-the-treasure*.

It is worth pausing to review Helen's and Rachel's decisions. Theirs is very much a style, a preference, expressed as a wish to make the game look better, rather than enhance the game by increasing the working components. It is easy – but in our view incorrect – to view this as somehow a lower or less sophisticated approach than that of the boys above[22]. On the contrary, in terms of the appearance of the screen, and its suggestiveness in contributing to the dialogue between the two children (and, potentially, their colleagues in Stockholm) the richness of the decoration makes a major contribution even if it does not make an equal contribution to the aspirations of the researchers! Yet even this turns out to need qualification.

At the workshop, Helen and Rachel sent their game via a long-distance bird to the Swedish children, Sara, Rebecka and Mattias. After they had played it, the Swedish children sent back a bird carrying the following message: 'What do you do with the animals?' They were clearly concerned that nothing happened on this scene, and they were unable to construct a narrative relating to the animals who were just sitting there.

When the Swedish children were interviewed about the game they confirmed that, despite flipping the objects to check, they couldn't determine the role of the animals as none displayed behaviours. They did not even appreciate that the new scene was 'an island' – to them it was just a circle. They were also worried that there was no portal out of the dragon scene, so once the player character was there, she was stuck:

> Int: Can you say what kind of changes they did to the original game? In the first game they sent to you compared to the original game?
>
> Mattias: They had changed the hamburger (scene). They made a path where the hamburger was so we entered that. And then you couldn't get out of there. It was a round circle that you couldn't get through. With animals.
>
> Int: Was it the last scene they had added?
>
> Sara: No, we couldn't get out of there. It was like a dead end.

Helen and Rachel did not perceive a problem about there being no behaviours – they were too deeply engaged with the narrative generated during the construction of their game. However, from a player's perspective, this lack of any description of the rules of the game was obviously a problem. What the Swedish children were asking for was some kind of explicit description of the player rules,

Figure 10: The Dragon Island scene, with animated pictures but no behaviours or portals.

possibly in terms of system rules, and how these would benefit the narrative of the game. The Swedish children chose not to substitute system rules for player rules (maybe because they were unsure of the narrative), but they did suggest that the new scene should be connected to another scene. This would involve creating a system rule by copying an object from another part of the game, which might, in turn, clarify the narrative of the game as a whole.

When we interviewed both sets of children about their activities at the end of the workshop, there was unanimous agreement that sending and receiving games and comments via long distance birds and chatting via video-conferencing was the best part of the day – nobody seemed to mind the language problem. They especially emphasised that receiving games was very exciting. The Swedish children claimed that the game they received was much better than their own game, but when we pushed them a little, they were articulate in their criticism:

Int: Mattias, do you think your game was better?

Mattias: I don't think it was better

Int: Rebecka, didn't you didn't think it was better?

Rebecka: I think it was worse I think it was better as it was. That dragon just stood there. It didn't do anything

Mattias: No

Int: The dragon did ...

Sara: They had not done anything new. Just added pictures.

After the children had overcome their initial politeness, it became clear that they were unenthusiastic about the English girls' scene. They emphasised that the animals on the Dragon Island did nothing that contributed to their idea of the game, and in particular, they were critical of the lack of system rules (see Sara's final comment) that would benefit the game as a whole. It seems that the Swedish

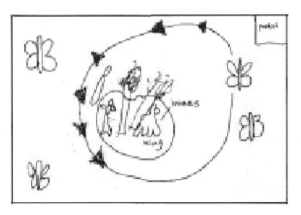

Figure 11. Helen and Rachel's plan for a new scene

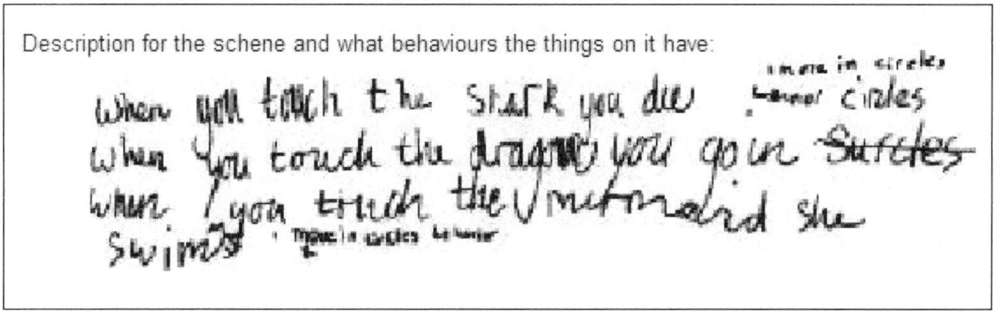

Description for the schene and what behaviours the things on it have:

Figure 12. Description of the scene and the behaviours needed to create it.

children were firmly of the opinion that in order for a new object to have any point, it must have system rules underlying it – perhaps unsurprisingly, as there was no possibility of accessing any implicit player rules that the constructors may have had in mind when they created it.

Adding some behaviours to the new scene

In the aftermath of the workshop, the English girls started work on a new version of their Dragon Island scene. Perhaps their new found enthusiasm was stimulated by the Swedish girls' lukewarm reception of their previous attempts – we cannot be sure. The researcher asked them to plan their scene on paper, in order to negotiate with each other a clear view of what each had in mind, and in subsequent sessions they worked on constructing the scene and adding it to the adventure game. The initial sketch is shown in Figure 11.

We also asked Helen and Rachel to write down a description of their scene and the behaviours it would have. They were extremely lucid about what should happen, and which behaviours the objects would need to make them work (the text is re-presented in the caption in Figure 12).

> When you touch the shark you die. When you touch the dragon you go in circles (I move in circles behaviour). When you touch the mermaid, she swims (move in circles behaviour).

Helen and Rachel chose a new background for their scene and proceeded to add functionality to objects within it – this time without any help at all. They added a behaviour to the shark so it would move in a square and another to the butterflies so they would 'fly' around in elliptical orbits. These behaviours were supposed to indicate 'guarding'. But they did add one system rules that guarded quite explicitly. They added a second dragon, identical to the one that was simply animated except that it was 'dangerous'. It had been given a disappearing be-

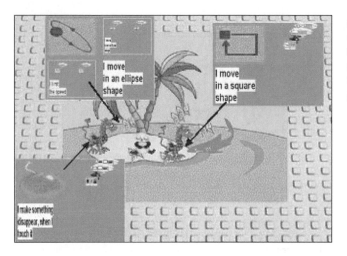

Figure 13. The final Dragon Island scene showing the behaviours on the flip side of the pictures

haviour, so that it would blow up anything that touched it – including the player character (see Figure 13).

We have no detailed records of the Swedish children's reaction to these changes but we do know that they found out which object they had to avoid to achieve their goal.

Concluding remarks

The first episode illustrates how Jacob and Ricard were unable to appreciate the rich narrative that Sarah and Jane had ascribed to the characters in the space scene, because of the lack of system rules, or – it must be said – a shared natural language. The lack of a shared interpretation of the player rules had made it impossible to appreciate the game in the way the English girls had intended. In the second episode, although Helen and Rachel were initially satisfied with their new scene, they subsequently realised that they needed to add some system rules to their game in order to satisfy the demands of their (remote) collaborators. The catalyst for this was undoubtedly the collaboration with the children in Sweden, and in particular, the difficulty of the Swedish children – communicated in their disappointment – in understanding the point of the 'enhancements': Without any new system rules, they couldn't possibly understand the constructors' narrative. For the English children the enhancements stood for themselves, as part of a new narrative with an attractive set of objects. We should not underestimate this: Even adding a new scene which does not seem to add to the richness of the play, adds complexity and can engage the programmer with non-trivial ideas. Adding two dragons, one dangerous and one not, for instance, adds risk and excitement to the narrative. But this could not be communicated to the Swedish children.

Here is the crux of both episodes. In a face-to-face setting, all the children would have probably been enthusiastic about the new narrative, and would have agreed behaviours that would convey that narrative. The remoteness of the two groups of children forced a need for formalisation, and this was felt initially by the Swedes, and subsequently appreciated by the English children in the second episode. Of course much had changed between the workshop and the subsequent activities: the children were more experienced (time is an important determinant of outcomes), they had received the negative feedback, and were encouraged by the researchers to plan their scene on paper (a not insignificant intervention). Neither can we argue that system rules necessarily stand for themselves: the introduction of new portals, for example, may well need informal communication to assist in understanding the narrative behind the idea. Nevertheless, the episodes reported above do lend credence to the conjecture that the distributed character of the games workshop made the distinction between player and system rules more salient and supported the children in these transformations.

More generally, the two episodes described suggest ways in which our initial observations can be elaborated. First, we have seen how game-*play* is not antithetical to game-*construction* – on the contrary, provided sufficient care is given to the design of the system, they can be mutually constitutive. We suggest that the tension between play and creativity with which we began, can be resolved even at this young age and, possibly, alongside significant learning outcomes concerned with the formalisation of rule systems. There was clearly creativity in making the imaginary situation overt and appreciating how the rules governed the constructed game. While the episodes described here do no more than illustrate the possibilities, we propose that this area is worthy of further investigation (now taking place in a follow-up project entitled *WebLabs* – see www.weblabs.eu.com).

Second, we also suggest that Piaget's claims that formal elaboration of game rules only develops at age 11-12 may need to be viewed differently. Nothing in Piaget's theory rules out the possibility that some precocious children may adopt strategies uncharacteristic of their age-range. But studies such as Playground, where children work together in virtual communities, may encourage greater account to be taken of the mediating role of the tools at hand, and especially the distinctive character of online communication with a non-textual but formal means to express relationships between objects.

Chapter Five

The KidStory Project: developing collaborative storytelling tools for children, with children

Danaë Stanton[1], **Claire O'Malley**[1], **Victor Bayon**[1],
Juan-Pablo Hourcade[2], **Yngve Sundblad**[3], **Carina Fast**[3],
Sue Cobb[1], **Gustav Taxén**[3], **Steve Benford**[1]

[1] *Mixed Reality Laboratory, University of Nottingham*
[2] *Human-Computer Interaction Lab, University of Maryland, USA*
[3] *The Royal Institute of Technology, Stockholm*

This chapter presents work carried out within the EU-funded KidStory project. The project involved the design, development and evaluation of technology to support collaborative storytelling among groups of young children. One of the main aims of the project was to develop tools that were inherently collaborative. This required developing new approaches to the design of shared software and hardware interfaces. Conventional computer hardware was replaced with tangible and reactive interfaces to produce shared storytelling objects and shared augmented spaces. Key to the project was the integration of this technology into real classroom environments and teaching practices. The KidStory project implemented a co-operative design approach in the development of the technologies, involving children and teachers directly as inventors and design partners. This process resulted in technology being developed that was tailored to the needs of children and teachers in the school environment. From an educational perspective, our goal was to develop technologies that supported collaboration and storytelling skills. Evaluation studies examined the effect of multiple input devices and tangible interfaces on children's collaborative behaviour, the nature of children's storytelling with and without technology and the development of children's storytelling ability. The chapter concludes by outlining the project legacy and briefly describing the ongoing work in this area.

The vision – an augmented room in a box

The KidStory vision was to develop technologies to augment a space for story-telling that could be packed away in a box and pulled out again by teachers in the course of a school day. The contents of the box would enable the use of physical artefacts, with digital information, to create an imaginative environment in which stories could be created, told or performed. Inherent in this idea was that the technology would be designed with children and teachers to be easily integrated within the classroom.

Introduction

Interactive story environments had already been developed. What was new about KidStory was that children would be authoring the stories. For example, the MIT KidsRoom allowed children to collaboratively discover a hidden story (Bobick *et al*, 1999). In Druin and Perlin (1994), rooms were designed to tell a story for visitors to experience. These immersive rooms consisted of physical objects that were used as input to a program that controlled lights, sound and video. The storytelling environments developed in the KidStory project aimed to provide a creative authoring environment as well as an environment to be experienced by others and presented to an audience.

Both children and teachers participated in designing the collaborative tools for storytelling. The two schools involved were in Nottingham, England, and in Stockholm, Sweden. The children were aged between 5 and 7. Our design methods with children were derived from cooperative inquiry (Taxén *et al,* 2001, Druin, 1999), a methodology that combines and adapts the low-tech prototyping of participatory design (Bødker, Ehn, Kyng, Kammersgaard, Sundblad, 1987, Greenbaum and Kyng, 1991, Schuler and Namioka, 1993), the observation and note-taking techniques of contextual inquiry (Beyer and Holtzblatt, 1998) and the time and resources of technology immersion (Druin *et al*, 1999).

The ultimate goal of all design sessions was to generate new or refine existing technology design ideas. Sessions with an educational design were combined with sessions that evaluated existing related technologies. Together, they provided the children with a framework for thinking critically about technology and helped both children and adults develop a common language and terminology for technology and design. The suggestions for improvements that resulted were either used directly to make changes to existing pieces of technology (e.g., KidPad) or were fed into brainstorming sessions where ideas for new technology were generated and/or elaborated upon (particularly during the second and third year of the project). The brainstorming ideas were further analysed by the adult researchers and a number of them were selected for implementation. A number of prototypes that implemented the ideas were then built and brought back to the school for further refinement. This iteration loop continued over a number of cycles.

Over the course of the project the technologies evolved from multiple input devices at a shared desktop computer to tangible interfaces and finally towards distributed augmented spaces. The use of these technologies, by both children and teachers, was evaluated by experiments, observational studies and interviews. The main focus of the evaluation studies was collaborative behaviour and story-telling with the technology. There were three phases to the project.

In the first phase, the desktop version of KidPad, a collaborative storytelling tool for children, was extended to enable simultaneous use of multiple input devices. Usually two or three children developed a story together at a desktop computer. Evaluation studies of the use of two mice examined collaborative behaviour when two children could control the input at the same time.

In the second phase of the project the technology was scaled up to create an aug-mented storytelling environment. KidPad was displayed on large screens and a number of tangible interfaces were developed that enabled children to work in groups to create and retell stories. As stated above, throughout the project both the children and teachers were part of the research team involved in the design, development and evaluation of the technology. Evaluation over the first two years of the project found that children involved in designing and developing story-telling environments produced better-developed stories than their peers.

In phase three, a number of the newly developed technologies were integrated, to develop augmented spaces for shared storytelling. A range of configurations were tested. A usability study of one of these set-ups examining the collaborative behaviour of the children over three sessions revealed the importance of im-mediate feedback and visibility of action for effective collaboration to take place.

Multiple input devices and Single Display Groupware

The first phase of the project focused on extending the traditional desktop com-puter using software tools for collaborative storytelling. The software environ-ment used throughout the project was a system called KidPad.

KidPad provides drawing, typing and hyperlinking capabilities in a large, zoom-able, two-dimensional canvas. It supports collaboration by accepting input from multiple mice. To support shoulder-to-shoulder collaboration, KidPad uses an approach called single-display groupware (SDG), where an application that uses one display accepts input from multiple devices, each controlled by a user (Stewart *et al*, 1999). In order to support this approach in the user interface

KidPad uses local tools (Bederson *et al*, 1996). Local tools act as cursors and hold their own mode (e.g., a red crayon local tool draws red). Multiple local tools may be active at the same time, with each user controlling one tool. To change tools, users simply click on an unused tool to pick it up, or on another user's tool to make an exchange. By holding their own mode, local tools avoid the difficulties that arise with menus and palettes that rely on global modes when supporting multiple users (see figure 14).

Children were involved in design sessions to develop new functionality for the KidPad software. One of the key design features of the shared desktop version of KidPad was the concept of *encouraging* (rather than just supporting) collaboration. (This became a theme throughout the further technical developments in subsequent years.) The aim was to provide opportunities for children to discover the positive benefits of working together, for example by being able to create new graphics and effects for their stories (Benford *et al*, 2000). Encouraging collaboration is more proactive than merely *enabling* it. Something new is gained by choosing to work together, although the children may work independently if they wish. On the other hand, it is not as rigid as *enforcing* collaboration, for example by demanding that two children have to synchronise their actions in order to succeed, an approach that has been tried before with some positive gains in terms of individual development (e.g. Light *et al*, 1987). By encouraging collaboration we combined the educational goal of learning collaboration skills with our design philosophy of giving children some control.

In redesigning KidPad to encourage collaboration our basic approach was to support tool 'mixing'. By this we mean that when two (or sometimes more) children each use mixable tools at about the same time and place, the tools give enhanced functionality. As a concrete example of this approach, consider the operation of the crayons in KidPad. The initial version provided three colours. A frequent design suggestion from the children was to provide more colours. We immediately added three more crayons, but this was not enough. Our final solution was to enable children to collaborate and combine their crayons to produce new colours. If two children draw with two crayons close together, it results in a filled area between the two crayons whose colour is the mix of the two. In this case, the children are not prevented from drawing individually, but they gain additional benefits (new colours and filled areas) by working together.

We built in mixing capability for multiple uses of most of the local tools. In each instance, we added a 'special behaviour' that acts as if it is a natural extension of the behaviour with a single user. For example, with the collaborative version of the arrow tool, instead of moving the object selected, two or more children can squash and stretch selected drawing objects. Likewise, whilst the hand browser

Figure 14. KidPad in use with two mice

enables a single user to pan the story left and right, up and down, the collaborative version enables two or more children to zoom in and out by moving their hands apart or closer together (see Benford *et al*, 2000 for more details).

Kidpad's hyperlinking capabilities benefit children by giving them the ability to create links from a drawing to any other drawing or view of the KidPad canvas. When children follow a link, the screen animates to show the target drawing or view. Children use these linking capabilities to create and tell stories. They draw scenes in KidPad's zoomable space, link them together, and then follow the links to tell the story. KidPad also supports non-linear stories, as one scene may have more than one link coming out of it, giving users the ability to experience the story through different paths.

In a study comparing KidPad to other media, KidPad's animation and zooming capabilities were found to aid storytelling. Boltman *et al* (2002) asked children to view a wordless book and tell the story to adults as they moved through the images. The children viewed the story in one of three forms: on paper, using traditional hyperlink (which consists of no animation or zooming) or using KidPad. Seventy-two 7-year old children took part in the study. After looking at the wordless book, participants performed one of two tasks. The first examined elaboration and involved children retelling the story, a page at a time. The second task was for children to recall the story without any materials. The structure of the stories was examined (text length, references to advancing plots etc.) and story content analysed (relationships, events, goals.) and this revealed that children in the KidPad group demonstrated more complex structure in their stories and had greater discussion about initiating events.

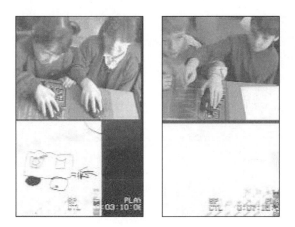

Figure 15. Two-mice pair
Figure 16. Shared-mouse pair

A classroom-based evaluation study was carried out to examine the process of children's collaboration when they use one or two mice at a desktop computer (see figures 15 and 16). Pairs of children worked together to re-create a poem in pictorial format. In-depth qualitative examination of interaction using 'collaboration networks' highlighted the differences in working styles in response to the different conditions. Children using two mice divided up their task, worked in parallel, and showed limited reciprocity and elaboration of ideas. Children sharing one mouse demonstrated varied behaviours ranging from highly collaboratively work to extreme domination by one partner (Stanton and Neale, in press). Analysis of the story quality produced by these children found a higher quality of stories produced by the children using two mice. Interaction with shared input devices also led to greater equity between the different gender pairings, whereas interaction with only one input device led to poorer performance in mixed gender and male pairs. Analysis of the dialogues showed that the different gender pairings displayed very different styles of work. Only the female pairs used the type of discussion that characterises collaborative work (Abnett *et al*, 2001).

Towards the end of phase one KidPad became integrated into the classroom for paired work and for whole class teaching.

Storytelling objects and tangible interfaces

While in phase one, multiple input devices at the desktop were seen to facilitate pairs of children in actively working on a shared task, the aim of phase two was to extend our technology to support large groups of children. We also wanted to incorporate classroom materials into the set-up, to enable teachers and children to move more seamlessly between these materials and technology.

Accordingly, in phase 2, tangible and physical interfaces were explored: The aim was to break with the conventional computer hardware and find new ways of interacting that were more natural, more collaborative and more easily integrated into a classroom setting. As KidPad was being used in our schools as part of mainstream teaching, we chose to focus on interfaces for retelling KidPad stories. Two main considerations were taken into account in phase 2 development:

- *Group size*: KidPad on laptops seemed to work well for small groups (2-3 children) but not so well for larger groups. We needed an alternative approach to scale up to support collaboration in larger groups, potentially involving the whole class

- *Story retelling versus story creation*: KidPad has so far been focused mainly on supporting story creation. We wished to extend its capability to support story retelling and the performance or enactment of stories to watching audiences

A central idea and objective in KidStory was to design technology with children and teachers as partners in a cooperative design process, thus fostering technology development. The main design methods and activities used with teams of children, teachers and researchers in the KidStory project were:

- Contextual Inquiry with observations of what participants do with technologies they currently have.

- Co-operative (Participatory) Design, where teams of adults and children collaboratively create low-tech prototypes out of paper, clay, glue, crayons, and so on.

- Personal design journals, where children have entered drawings and texts.

Figure 17. Co-operative design session in the classroom

Figure 18. Children working on a prototype of a storytelling machine

- Working Prototype Introduction in Schools, not as finished products, but as works-in- progress, asking participants for their suggestions and ideas.

- Design and Development Workshops at Laboratories ('Invasions'), concentrated events over 1-2 weeks at partners´ laboratories, for focused final design and technical development.

By applying these methods, the partners come to know each other and their views of technology in various ways. It helped to establish a partnership between the children and adults and encouraged the research participants to begin to think and act as technology designers and evaluators. These methods can be used to gather data, develop prototypes and stimulate new research directions and they become mechanisms for input into the technology design process (see figure 17).

There was a gradual change in focus in the work in KidStory as the partners became more and more accustomed to the design practices and to working together as critics, designers, and inventors.

The combination of observation, low-tech prototyping and time-intensive technology design sessions has led to the successful development of new prototypes (see figure 18).

Working with the children in phase 2, we prototyped 'storytelling machines' which led to new ideas for tangible technologies. We can point to a number of specific ideas of storytelling objects and storytelling rooms that we can trace through co-operative design with low-tech prototypes, through technical prototypes into further extensions into new designs.

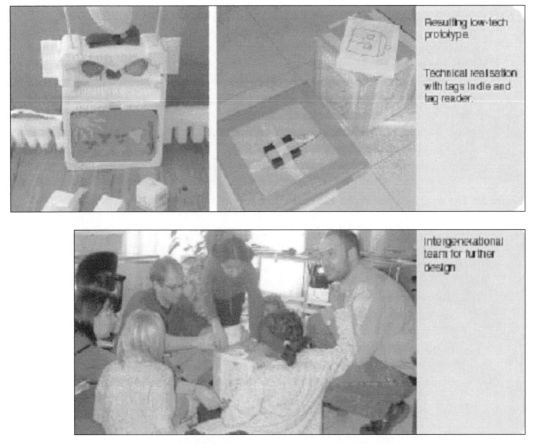

Resulting low-tech prototype.

Technical realisation with tags inside and tag reader.

Intergenerational team for further design

Figure 19 a, b, c. The development of the storydice from low tech storytelling prototype to tangible interface

Figure 19 illustrates such a process for the storytelling dice, invented by an 8-year-old girl in Rågsved as partner in a co-operative design group with four children and two adults.

Other physical and tangible interfaces were also developed (see figures 20 and 21). These included: the aforementioned Storydice (physical dice that could be placed on a surface in order to trigger graphical and sonic effects in KidPad); A Magic Sofa (children could sit in different locations on the sofa and this took them to different locations on screen) and a Magic Carpet (a series of pressure mats that groups of children could use to collectively navigate around a story that was being projected onto a screen). In order to build these prototypes, we explored a variety of underlying interaction technologies including the use of Radio Frequency ID (RFID) tags and barcodes to tag physical objects, the use of pressure switches, and the potential for video tracking of simple group gestures.

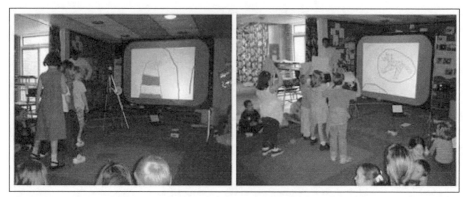

Figure 20. The magic carpet in use with camera tracking

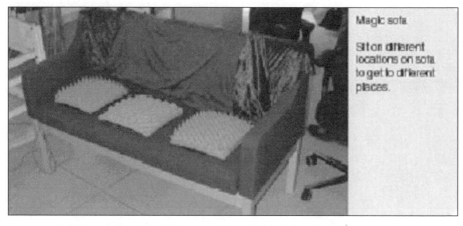

Figure 21. Magic sofa prototype (with RFID tags under foam pads)

Some of these interfaces were explicitly designed to encourage collaborative behaviour, for example, the magic carpet al lowed increased speed of movement through story elements when several children used the carpet and more sensors were pressed.

Interviews with teachers and children during this phase of the project indicated that teachers had seen improvements in the children participating in the project compared with other class groups in the school. Teachers noted improvements in communication and presentation skills, self-confidence and self-esteem. More-over, the teachers involved in the project also reported that their own self-esteem and confidence with technology had improved as a result of working with the project. This had spread beyond the teachers who were directly participating in the project and an awareness of how Information Technology can be used to support and achieve other educational goals (not just supporting IT lessons) grew right across the school.

One of the challenges of the KidStory project was that, being based within real school environments, our school activities had to integrate with other activities going on at the school. Sometimes we were given a very short time to run sessions, on occasion only a few children were available to work with us, and at times we had to work while performing other teaching activities. Thus a degree of flexibility was essential to the success of our integration within the school environments (see Stanton *et al,* 2001). Activities planned at project meetings had to allow flexibility in execution 'on the ground'.

The development of prototypes of Shared Storytelling Objects, which the children used to retell their stories created in KidPad, produced a change in children's interview responses at the end of year 2. At the end of year 1 the children had not mentioned storytelling but focused much more on technology design, whereas at the end of year 2 the KidStory group talked about innovative ways of writing and telling stories.

Augmented space for shared storytelling

In phase three of the project the aim was to scale up to larger room-sized environments to explore how new storytelling technologies might be deployed throughout a whole classroom. We were aiming towards the more general toolkit for the classroom that children and teachers might easily reconfigure for different purposes, rather than creating a particular pre-defined configuration, such as the magic carpet. These phase three developments have built on the work described in phase two by focusing on the following key issues:

- *Integration with traditional materials* – in taking account of the physical classroom context, we wished to create technologies that made use of, and integrated traditional materials (e.g., paper, cardboard models, costumes). The technology could thus be used as part of larger classroom projects rather than an isolated activity.

- *Creativity awareness* – we noted during the observations that children seldom had the right tools to express themselves. For instance some children had problems drawing with the mouse, producing poor definition and quality drawings. Tools must be designed that let children express their ideas. A mouse is not necessarily the best tool for drawing.

- *Component based* – tools should be plugged, used and put away as required.

- *Space adaptable* – teachers and children should be able to use the devices in different spatial configurations, for instance on the children's workspaces, tables, floor, stage room, etc. The PC and the magic carpet required specific locations.

Figure 22. Children drawing on paper and with pda

• *Scalability* – KidPad and the magic carpet scaled from two to four children. The technology should be designed with classroom scalability in mind so more children can participate in the creation or retelling experiences.

We tried to address some of these issues with a variety of technologies in the integrated set-ups. Some of these are described below:

Image Scanner: Scalable Input

The scanner provided an easy means to integrate real drawings into KidPad stories. As pen and paper are readily available in classrooms, they can be used as scalable input devices for creating digital content and a scanner used as a gateway. Paper and crayons were distributed around the space. Children drew on pieces of paper, then went to the scanner, pressed the button, and the drawing was scanned and uploaded into KidPad.

Pda Crayons: Digital Input

The KidPad interface has six crayons of different colours among its local tools. These can be picked up, used, and dropped using the mice. We designed an application for Pda (Personal Digital Assistants) that emulated the six different KidPad crayons using six different Pdas, each colour-labelled and representing one colour. The content could draw on the Pda off-line and be 'dropped' to KidPad via infrared beaming to an infrared port plugged to the computer rendering KidPad. In this case, any Pda could be picked up, used, shared and dropped, just like real crayons (see figure 22).

Web Camera: Photographs

A Webcam was attached to KidPad. When children took a picture, whatever was in focus was uploaded into KidPad as an image.

Sound: Story Effects

During the first two years of the project, children suggested that they wanted ways of recording and playing sounds in their stories. Sound recording and replaying provided an easy and enjoyable way for children to integrate voice/ sound effects and even full narrations of events to their stories. By placing a RF-ID Tag on the tag reader any sound picked up by the microphone was recorded till the tag was removed. When the tag was removed a bar-coded label was automatically printed and this could be pasted anywhere. To replay the sound, children just had to scan the barcode with the barcode reader.

Moving technology into a larger space, providing room for objects to become organised spatially, means that other people's actions are made more visible. So we did not include features that would explicitly encourage collaboration in these new technology configurations.

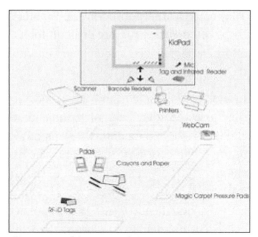

Figure 23. Diagram of the tangible set up

A study was carried out to examine collaboration on a story creation task using one configuration of these technologies. Four children used tangible technologies over three sessions. The technology consisted of a large visual display to which children could input content (using Pdas and a scanner), record sounds (using RF-ID tags) and navigate around the environment using the magic carpet. They could then retell their story using bar-coded images and sounds (see figure 23). The three sessions were video recorded and analysed (see figure 24). There were many instances of children helping one another, predicting someone else's actions and coming to their aid and developing strategies to overcome any problems with elements of the technology. For example by moving the carpet a little it is possible to see that the link has worked. In this example, Sam seemed to plan ahead and realise what needed to be done:

Elaine and Joanne have made a link. Elaine is waiting for the link to print out. Sam goes quietly to the carpet and moves it just a little to the side. When the link prints Sam suggests Elaine check the link using the barcode reader. Elaine does so and it works.

As the pace of the interaction is relatively slow and visible, children could observe the actions of one another and react to them.

Figure 24. A group of children working together to create a story

They could learn by observing one another. Additionally, the physical distribution of the set-up makes it more difficult for a child to work alone in terms of physical effort and time taken to complete a task. Over the sessions and within each one the complexity of their collaborative behaviours grew (see Stanton *et al,* 2002).

In another longitudinal study (Fast and Kjellin, 2001) children's storytelling skills were assessed at the beginning and end of the project. This study examined how children's storytelling ability developed while participating in storytelling activities over the course of two years. The experimental group consisted of twelve children aged 5 years at the start of the study and 7 at the end. The control data was taken of twelve 7 year old children who had not taken part in KidStory activities but attended usual classroom activities instead. The KidStory sessions consisted of listening to stories, dramatising familiar stories, retelling stories, creating prototypes and design ideas for technology, creating stories together in small or large groups in KidPad, creating novel stories using the Storydice and documenting their work in journals. Pre- and post tests consisted of children being told an identical story and then asked to create a story themselves. The data was analysed on six categories of story development. Stories created by the experimental group were found to be more developed than their earlier stories and those produced by the control group. The experimental group was also found to be better able to answer the question explicitly.

The results indicated a significant improvement in the quality of children's stories at the end of the project. This is to be expected since at the age of 5 children are at an important developmental stage anyway. However, the study did identify significantly higher quality of stories created by the 7-year old children at the Swedish school involved in the KidStory project compared with matched 7-year olds from the same school who had not been involved in the project. It was interesting to note that, in this study, the KidStory children involved themselves in their stories significantly more often at the end of the project (80%) than at the beginning (22%) and also more than older children who had not been involved in the project (33%). Moreover, these stories involving personal experiences were qualitatively better than those without. We conclude that children's creativity was stimulated by their involvement in the KidStory project through the attention that was placed on problem solving through storytelling in the Stockholm School sessions.

The researchers' observations of the children's activities during KidStory sessions and the interviews with teachers indicate several areas where children's development was supported by the KidStory project. The teachers noted that the children's confidence and self-esteem had been enhanced by working with the KidStory team.

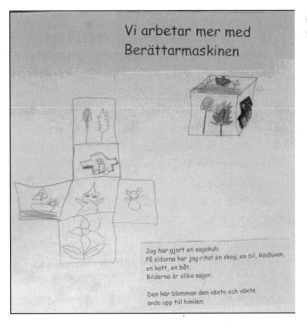

Vi arbetar mer med
Berättarmaskinen

Jag har gjort en sagokub.
På sidorna har jag ritat en skog, en bil, Rödluvan,
en katt, en båt.
Bilderna är olika sagor.

Den här blomman den växte och växte
ända upp till himlen.

Figure 25. The storytelling dice in the inventor's journal

The Nottingham children's communication and presentation skills had developed, due in part to their frequent presentations to the class. The KidStory classes had gained from having increased computer resources in the classroom and the children readily used the variety of technologies and interfaces to create and tell stories. They showed little difficulty in understanding or using the technology. The KidStory children had more experience of working in pairs and groups and this improved their collaboration skills. One Nottingham teacher told us how impressed she was by the children's ability to work collaboratively and she now includes more collaborative tasks in her classroom teaching. The researchers observed all the teachers involved in the KidStory project had developed much greater awareness, experience and confidence with technology.

The teachers also benefited from the relationship between the school and the research team. The headteacher felt that this helped to raise the children's awareness of other educational institutions (e.g. universities). The teachers noted the benefits to children of keeping journals of their design activities in the project (see figure 25). A study carried out in Sweden examined journal entries made by children over the three years of the project. From autumn 1998 to spring 2001, twenty-seven children were asked to draw or write their reflections in a personal bound paper journal after every design activity. These were analysed to examine children as learners, critics, inventors and technology design partners (see Druin and Fast, 2002).

Conclusions and Legacy

One of the most successful aspects of the KidStory project was the uptake of technology in the schools. Within the first year of the project the teachers requested that we leave KidPad permanently in the classroom and they included a daily time slot for its use. In Sweden and in the UK, KidStory technology was successfully integrated within our partner schools and, at their request, remained in the schools after the project ended. Other teachers in the schools have also started to use the technology and parents in Nottingham and Stockholm have downloaded KidPad from the website for their children to use at home. Our studies have identified clear evidence for strengthening the abilities of pupils as inventors/design partners and as storytellers and enhancing teachers' confidence in using IT generally and to support collaborative storytelling.

Public and media interest in the project has been strong and recognition of the value of the schools-based technology development approach has been endorsed by the education review body in the UK (see Ofsted report, 2001). In Stockholm a main impact on the community has been through media and fair presentations of KidStory as an example for the political committees responsible for education, of what can be achieved through cooperation between interdisciplinary research and regular schools. The KidPad software has also been featured in three exhibitions at the Museum of Science and Technology in Stockholm, of which one is a touring exhibition ('Sm@rt on Tour') that has visited several countries in Europe and is being displayed in several Swedish cities.

While the research products would not fit easily into a box, or at least, not a small one (see Bayon *et al*, 2002), the project achieved all its other objectives and the legacy lives on in on-going projects. KidStory partners from Nottingham are involved in the playing and learning theme within the Equator project funded by EPSRC. Both Nottingham and KTH are involved the EU Disappearing Computer project Shape, which involved KidStory themes in its second living exhibition at Nottingham castle. The project interLiving, 2001-2003, within the EU Disappearing Computer initiative, has as its theme 'Designing Interactive, Intergenerational Interfaces for Living Together'. It is co-ordinated by one of the KidStory partners, KTH in Stockholm, and includes longitudinal (three year) contacts and design sessions with three families (eight households) in each of greater Stockholm and greater Paris. It is clearly inspired by KidStory in theme, partners and methods (Beaudouin-Lafon *et al*, 2002). The KidStory work from the third year has also been extended into StoryRooms, a toolkit that allows children to design their own reactive, mixed-reality spaces (Alborzi *et al*, 2002).

> 'The success of KidStory relies on the working partnership of the project partners, on collaboration and on achieving a mutual goal.' (Teacher, UK)

> 'KidStory is an inventor school, where we work together.' (Child, Sweden)

Acknowledgements

This work was conducted as part of the KidStory project funded under the ESPRIT I[3] Experimental Schools Environment initiative (#29310). We gratefully acknowledge the contribution of other project members at the University of Nottingham, SICS and KTH in Sweden and The University of Maryland, USA particularly H. Neale, J. Wilson, R. Ingram, A. Ghali, A. Boltman, A. Druin, B. Bederson, K. Åkesson, P. Hansson, J. Humble, M. Kjellin, K. Simsarian. Thanks also to the teachers and children at both our participating schools: Rågsvedsskolan, Stockholm and Albany Infants School, Nottingham.

Chapter Six

Children's playful learning with a robotic construction kit

Augusto Chioccariello, Stefania Manca, Luigi Sarti[23]
Istituto per le Tecnologie Didattiche – C.N.R.
Genova, Italy

Introduction

Robotic constructions offer the opportunity to explore a class of cognitively relevant concepts such as emerging behaviours, theory of control, etc. The overall aim of our research was to assess the suitability of a robotic construction kit for young children (age 5 to 8). Could children of this age build and program robots on their own? If so, what kind of activities, tools, environments are best suited for the task?

To this end, we focused on two distinct but parallel approaches: the LEGO Mind-Storms kit was partially redesigned to increase the typologies of possible constructions (through the design of new sensors, actuators and pre-assembled mechanical components). A programming language was designed that is context specific and extensible, and is therefore capable of facing a range of problems that are tightly related to the typologies of activity for which it has been pre-disposed. This chapter describes the theoretical background, the adopted research methodology, the evolution of the physical play material, the features of the programming environment, and case studies that present selected findings of the field-testing. Possible evolutions of the work are outlined that would enable children to build and program robots in less supportive contexts.

This chapter describes the work carried over within the *Construction kits made of Atoms and Bits project* (CAB) (Askildsen *et al,* 2001a), whose objective was to explore and investigate the relationships and attitudes of young children towards behaving objects.

The appeal of ideas such as building constructions that expose interactive autonomous behaviour to preschool and elementary school children was a central aspect of our research. In particular the CAB project strived to:

- experiment with and validate a methodology which fosters children's interaction with computers through the use of cybernetic constructions
- encourage children aged 4 to 8 to approach and use cybernetic objects in play/explore contexts (see figure 26)
- investigate how the structure of learning processes develops when children encounter and experiment directly with multimedia while working with cybernetic constructions
- explore the possibility of making software and the play material more suited to young children.

From a functional point of view, the investigation of the relationship between young children and cybernetics could be broken down into the areas of play material, software and learning background/practice. This structure is reflected in the composition of the CAB consortium. While the LEGO Group Denmark, focused on the play materials, the Istituto per le Tecnologie Didattiche (ITD) in Italy investigated and designed programming environments, including support material (Askildsen *et al*, 2001b). The Högskolan för Lärarutbildning och Kommunikation (HLK) at Jönköping, Sweden, and the Comune di Reggio Emilia (CRE) in Italy anchored the research efforts to classroom evaluation of the material. They provided cognitive and educational interpretations of observed results that led to further improvements to the materials and methodology (CRE, 2001; Gustafsson and Lindh, 2001).

Constructionism stresses the role concrete objects play in the complex process of knowledge construction (Papert, 1980, 1993; Harel and Papert, 1991; Turkle and Papert, 1992). The traditional operational and experiential approach of *learning by doing* (Dewey, 1910) is therefore re-interpreted in light of the potential that the construction of objects has for learning: Knowledge emerges as a result of an active engagement with the world through the creation and manipulation of artefacts (tangible or not), e.g. sand castles, computer programs, LEGO constructions etc., that have relevant personal meaning and, above all, are objects to think with. Similarly important in constructionism is the negotiation of meaning in the social world, considered as a crucial component of children's cognitive development. Learning and intelligence emerge in the social groups where individuals interact and collaborate to build a common body of shared knowledge. Children act together with peers and older subjects, who can provide support and motivation in coping with new cognitive tasks (Resnick, 1996). In the constructionist framework computer programming has always played a special role, as it is considered a tool to 'think about thinking'. But what is the meaning of 'programming'? There is no simple answer to this question. Programming can be many things to many people, and not everyone agrees on its potential to foster human learning and development. To some, programming is about writing code, while to others it is a way of thinking (Papert, 1980). Some perceive its potential in helping children sharpen their thinking or become better 'scientists' (Resnick *et al,* 2000), while others stress its ability to foster human creativity (Edwards *et al,* 1998) and enhance self-expression (Maeda, 2000).

Programming is a Pygmalion of sorts: it becomes what you want it to be. To a scientist, for example, it turns into a tool to master the world (through simulation). To a poet, it serves to create fiction or build a virtual world. Designers use it as a dynamic modelling tool. Literary critics see it as a new form of literacy. And for the developmental psychologist the 'hidden' value of programming lies primarily in its ability to promote the exploration, expression, and reflection of children's 'budding' selves-in-relation (Ackermann, 2000). Thanks to their programmability and inspectionability, *robots* and *programmable bricks* are among digital toys that today offer especially interesting features. They impact on the way of thinking about life, as they position themselves on the boundary between the animate and the inanimate (Turkle, 1995). Toys that behave elicit novel ways of exploring relational issues, like agency and identity. Their hybrid nature makes it possible to play out the fine line between objectifying minds and animating

Fig. 26. Children playing with drawing robots.

things and to come to grips with the hardships that identity formation involves (Ackermann, 2000).

Cybernetic construction kits, conjugating the physical building of artefacts with their programming, can foster the development of new ways of thinking (Resnick *et al,* 1996) that encourage new reflections on the relationship between life and technology (Martin *et al,* 2000), between science and its experimental toolset (Resnick *et al,* 2000), between robot design and values and identity (Bers and Urrea, 2000). As constructionism supporters argue, thanks to these objects many concepts that are usually considered prerogative of adults, who can deal with symbolic and abstract knowledge, are made accessible and comprehensible for children too (Resnick *et al,* 1998; Resnick, 1998).

The research methodology
Cybernetic construction kits are nowadays absent from the practices and culture of young children. While Papert suggested that the programmable brick can be used by preschool children (Papert, 2000), the available material is currently inadequate for this age. We therefore had to choose whether to redesign the material first (designing for children) or to involve the children from the beginning in our development effort (designing with children). We chose the latter, beginning with the LEGO® MINDSTORMS™ Robotic Invention System that was commercialised just as the project started. This allowed us to provide the schools involved in the project with stable and reliable material. However, we were aware that such material would not be suitable for autonomous use by children. What happens when a product that has been designed for 12-year-olds becomes an educational object for 5-year-olds? How could such a choice be legitimated pedagogicaly? What has to be done to remove the factors that limit the accessibility to technology?

For the whole experimental phase, which lasted two years, we chose to include the children's activities with the programmable brick into the context and practice of everyday work. We followed the Reggio approach to early childhood education where special attention is paid to the development of meaningful learning contexts that facilitate the children's work. Activities are situated within projects that address a broad range of issues over an extended period of time; adults try to avoid acting invasively and yet know how to listen and document what goes on, striving to sustain the children's motivation (Malaguzzi, 1998).

The rationale of the experimental activities is therefore twofold: on the one hand, we consider the cognitive potential of toys as deeply anchored to the usage context and the culture that give them meaning. On the other hand, learning is seen as a social and contextualised process in which children receive support and scaffolding from adults in their exploration activities. The role of the teacher as a mediator of knowledge and skills was crucial for coping with the shortcomings of the available technology for this age group. The teachers also engaged in the documentation of children's activities as an integral part of their everyday work (Rinaldi, 1998). This documentation, produced in a variety of formats (texts, images, video, etc.), was made available to the entire CAB community.

The reflections and interpretations adults made on the issues that emerged from the work with the children, made it possible to consider the 'theories', albeit provisional, the children had developed during their experiments with LEGO Mind-Storms and with the subsequent versions of the construction kit. Our aim was to collect descriptive and narrative accounts of what happened in the encounters between the children and the construction kit and note how the situation developed. We saw the documentation as a process of reflection and elaboration that enabled us to elicit from the children the requirements for the evolution of the LEGO kit. The LEGO kit was incrementally modified according to these requirements through an iterative process.

Evolution of the play material

A typical LEGO construction contains some parts that are essential for its stability, some that provide extra abilities, and some that are purely decorative and meant to give the construction a certain character. To provide the best possible set of basic components in a construction kit a balance needs to be struck in the granularity of the components, maximising freedom in what can be constructed and at the same time minimising the intrinsic complexity. This is the trade-off between specific/powerful and generic/open-ended components. In the field-testing, most objects had to be designed and constructed by the teachers, thereby diminishing the meaning for the children of the constructions. The problems encountered can be clustered into three categories: the complexity of the LEGO Technic mechanical subsystem) the opaque design of sensors and actuators; the bias of the LEGO MindStorms kit toward mobile robots.

The mechanical subsystem

LEGO Technic is a flexible and powerful mechanical kit that enables experts to build complex robotic constructions. A rich body of literature is devoted to support adult users in mastering the complexity of this system (Martin, 1995; Ferrari and Ferrari, 2001).

Our approach was to identify and build pre-assembled mechanical modules aimed at improving children's autonomy in using the kit. Such sub-assemblies include a standard, ready-to-use vehicle chassis; a locomotion system with caterpillars; a structure to host a pair of contact sensors, to be used on a variety of

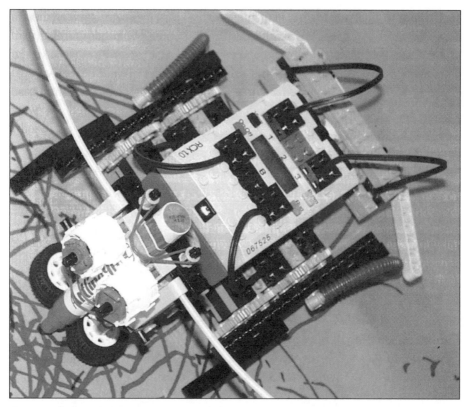

Figure 27. A vehicle assembled using the chassis, legs, a bumper with two touch sensors and a stub for holding a pen

vehicles; a conveyor belt; a motorised rotating cradle hosting the programmable brick.

This choice allowed children to include complex mechanics in their constructions, at the cost of restricting the creative exploration of the material (see Fig. 27). A better mechanical system for children should not start at the level of gears and axles but should abstract the different types of motions and make them combinable. The children could be provided with small modules that embed mechanical gear designs. This would allow them to investigate and apply a range of mechanisms, e.g. produce radial lever movements or translate high-torque rotation into faster low-torque, without having to build them from scratch.

Types of constructions

A construction kit, depending on the components it offers, inevitably favours some types of activity and hinders others, thus imposing an implicit bias on the typologies of allowed constructions. The LEGO MindStorms kit is designed to favour the construction of vehicles, mobile robots that interact with the environment. In order to encourage the development of other usage scenarios, further construction types were identified: 'kinetic sculptures' (the robot has moving mechanical parts, although it does not necessarily move around); 'animated constructions' (the robot features reactive behaviour using sound, light, messages etc.); 'cybernetic soft toys' (similar to Furbies, but easy to inspect and modify). Not all these proposals earned the children's and teachers' favour; some required a review and revision cycle or even abandonment. This was true of cybernetic soft toys, which caused more perplexity rather than acceptance among teachers, who were afraid to offer a pedagogically poor proposal.

The use of typologies other than vehicles reduces the need for complex mechanical constructions and allows for the exploration of reactive behaviours that fit, for instance, in storytelling, where we have observed children combine a variety of building material (LEGO, paper, fabric, clay). In these scenarios the reduced mechanical complexity lets children express their creativity and address the behaviour definition early in the construction process.

The design of active components: sensors and actuators

From discussion about construction types the need emerged to define additional sensors and actuator components. For example, children love to add recorded voice and sound to their computer-made artefacts. Accordingly, we designed and prototyped a tiny digital recorder that could 'give voice' to the robots. Other added components include: a light chain, a bend sensor, a sound sensor and an infrared transmitter. Having a variety of components each with its peculiar properties raises the issue of its readability: during the field-testing teachers often reported that it was difficult to explore the features of sensors and actuators, as the components did not communicate their functionality to the children. Following each phase of the field-testing, discussions about making materials more evocative and communicative led to suggestions for the improvement of their design. It would be desirable for sensors to be active: i.e., a sound sensor (microphone) could glow with differing intensity depending on the volume of sound it detects. The idea is to endow sensors with LEDs arranged in a line acting as a visual gauge. This solution would provide the children with a concrete reference level: as the sound rises in volume they would see an increased glow of the LEDs. This would be a step forward from the abstract numerical representation of sensor values currently displayed on the programmable brick.

Looking at design-functionality, we opted for an operational interface that was independent of the programmable brick: a button for recording and another for playing the sound are placed on the recorder itself. The prototype we produced allows for recording two short messages and can also be controlled program-matically. The experiments with the children, however, showed that they wanted both more and longer messages. One might privilege the interface transparency by associating just one component to each message: if longer messages are needed, one might always sequentially connect several recorders (Ananny, 2001). Such an approach allows for a story to be assembled by manipulating the order in which the various recorders are linked together. This enables complex interactions among sensors and sound sequences: for instance children could build a 'sound wall' that emits different sequences if the temperature rises above a certain level, if someone touches a hot-spot or if two bricks exchange a message. If the same features were to be available for vehicles, practical constraints would emerge on the weight and size of components, thus inducing the design of a single, smaller recorder, at the price of some opacity of its interface.

Building the robot's behaviour

Putting in the children's hands the tools to program the behaviour of a cybernetic construction is often questioned, since programming is not easy and many believe it should be left to specialists. If this were true, we should abandon the idea of a construction kit and limit ourselves to the design of cybernetic toys whose behaviour, although highly interactive, could not be modified by children.However, we believe that a kind of programming is indeed possible also for non-programmers, provided that it is supported by problem-specific tools (environment, language etc.).

The development of tools that make programming for specific problem solving accessible to people who are not particularly experienced (or interested) in computer science is a thriving research area. In particular work by Bonnie Nardi (1993) shows that users who are expert in a specific domain – or are interested in practicing it – can learn and manage formal languages relevant to that domain. Significant examples are tools such as spreadsheets or statistical analysis packages, which provide the user with a programming language to extend the system functionality. Tools of this type allow for the growth of a user population who, at various skill levels, benefit from the available programming functions.

To apply similar considerations to children, we have to assume that they can manage the level of complexity implicit in the control of robot behaviour. So it makes sense to set up a programming environment for children. In the CAB framework we have verified that children can indeed deal with robotic constructions, provided that the context is well structured.

What is the conceptual model that best supports the definition of robot behaviour? Let us start with a sample task: make a vehicle turn around a square-based obstacle. A beginner would probably think in terms of driving a car via a remote control, devising a solution in the imperative programming style of the Logo turtle: 'Go straight on along one side of the obstacle', 'Turn left 90 degrees' and 'Repeat these two instructions for the other three sides'. However, robots are endowed with sensors that 'perceive' the surrounding environment and allow them to react accordingly: programming a robot thus entails handling a number of sensors at the same time. The imperative programming style that is adequate for a broad range of situations (scientific computation, accounting, etc.) is inadequate for robot programming (Resnick, 1991; Papert, 1993).

If we add a touch sensor to our vehicle, for instance, we can address the problem in a radically different way: we can simulate the behaviour of a person who, in the darkness, has to circumnavigate an obstacle following its contour by hand. The program is built by relating the data coming from the sensors with the commands to the motors. A robot which 'touches' the wall as it goes on is hard to build with LEGO pieces; it is easier to make the vehicle oscillate bouncing in a zigzag fashion: the robot moves away from the wall when the sensor touches it and re-approaches it when the sensor loses the contact. In other words: 'if the sensor touches, turn on the motor on its side and turn off the one on the other side; if the sensor does not touch, turn its motor off and turn on the other one'.

A solution of this kind offers a number of advantages against the imperative approach: the behaviour emerges from the interaction between the robot and the obstacle, independently from the shape and size of the latter. Besides, this approach allows, with minimal morphological changes, for the solution of other problems. For instance, should we want the robot to follow a line on the floor, it would be enough to replace the touch sensor with a light sensor while keeping the same program structure: the robot will zigzag along the line contour. In all these cases, rather than representing the map of the world in the program, it is the 'playing field' that works as the map of itself (Brooks, 1991). In cases where the environment properties (the shape and size of the obstacle, the geometry of the line, etc.) are not known in advance the robot has to exhibit a level of adaptivity that can only be obtained through the use of sensors.

Domain orientation

We chose to represent the behaviour of a robot via a set of rules. A rule associates a condition (a test on the state of a sensor) with a sequence of actions (commands for the actuators), e.g. *if* the light sensor finds a high value of brightness *then* turn the motor on. The ease of using this rule system depends on the availability of conditions and actions that encapsulate the hardware details and are directly operational. The usability of conditions and actions in turn relies on assumptions on the type of construction. For instance, a vehicle with two motors can move for-

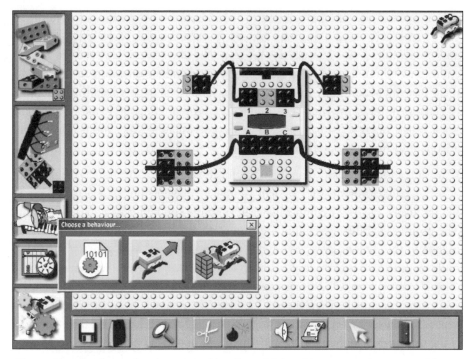

Figure 28a: A schematic representation of a vehicle with two touch sensors. The behaviour menu is selected, allowing for choice among the available behaviours that match the construction input and output set, or the definition of a new one.

ward and back, rotate left and right. Thus, turtle-like commands are provided for vehicles. For each construction type of which the programming environment is aware, a set of primitives is defined, that specialise the available functions to the problem at hand.

The overall behaviour of a construction emerges from the composition of simple behaviours that act concurrently. For example, a vehicle with touch sensors that moves in reaction to obstacles can be controlled by two behaviours. The first instructs the vehicle to move forward; when it touches an obstacle a second behaviour tells the robot to move back and turn in the direction opposite to the side of the collision.

Behaviours can be constructed and tested incrementally. If two or more behaviours are in charge of the same actuator, a priority mechanism decides which one is in control. In the last example, the behaviour that manages bumps has a higher priority than the one that moves the vehicle forward.

The programming environment presents a gallery of the existing projects and the possibility to start a new one. A project is composed of one or more construc-

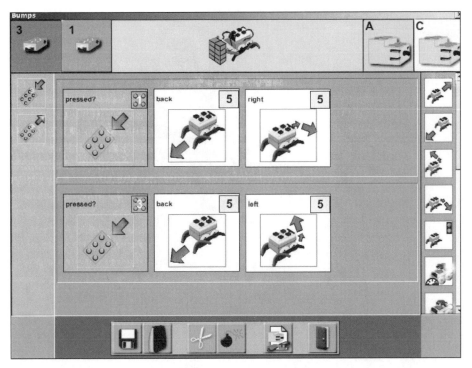

Figure 28b: The two rules that define the 'bump' behaviour. Note that only the conditions and actions associated with the selected input and output devices are shown

tions, and encompasses both the programs and a multimedia documentation of the children's work. The environment allows defining various types of construction to support the specialisation of programming components (behaviours, conditions, actions). A construction type makes certain assumptions on its mechanical components. A vehicle has a chassis equipped with two motors and is capable of moving and steering. When equipped with suitable sensors a vehicle can execute a range of built-in behaviours like 'follow a line', 'search for light', 'follow a wall', etc. The environment is capable of suggesting the possible behaviours available depending on what sensors are used in a given construction (Fig. 28a). When defining a new behaviour, only the conditions and actions that match the current hardware configuration are presented (Fig. 28b). Thanks to this specialisation mechanism, it is possible to let the environment evolve according to the specific needs of a project.

Tangible programming

A key challenge has been to empower children to construct their own programs out of physical components as they do with LEGO bricks. Tangible programming

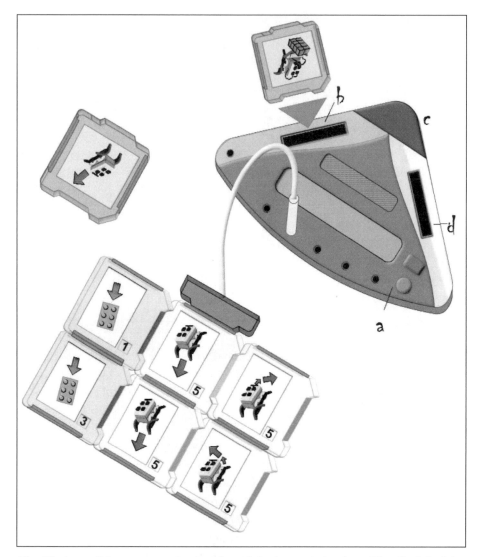

Fig. 29. A tangible programming version of the bump behaviour. The tiles' dock is annotated with labels indicating its features: a) conditions and actions tiles can be connected to this side of the dock to define a rule; b) the current rule can be used to define a new behaviour inserted in this slot, behaviours can be connected directly to this side; c) a communication device; d) an additional slot to redefine the meaning of a tile

(Suzuki and Kato, 1995) is an active field of research where many projects aim at young children (McNerney, 1999; Wyeth and Wyeth, 2001; Montemayor *et al,* 2002). The benefits of a tangible interface are twofold:

- it enables a small group of children to build programs together – unlike when using a screen-based programming environment where only one child at time can control the mouse or keyboard

- children can take advantage of the dexterity of their hands – in a graphical user interface objects are manipulated via a mouse or other suitable pointing devices.

Given the age of our target group, even small advantages are of value. A tangible version of the CAB programming environment, where behaviours, conditions and actions are themselves physical manipulative components of the kit, could realise the vision of mixing Atoms and Bits in a concrete and child friendly way. Fig. 29 provides an illustration of how this could be done using existing technology. The tiles contain electronic components, each with their own ID, and once connected are capable of communicating their topology (Gorbet *et al,* 1998). A tiles dock reads the tile configuration, generates a program and downloads it into the programmable brick. The dock also communicates with a computer to connect the tangible interface with the one on the screen. The kit can be extended to redefine the meaning of a tile.

The computer would still offer distinct advantages, for example in storing and documenting previous work or exchanging behaviours at a distance, but would not be required to start a project.

Metacognitive and social support

We feel that software which can retain a memory of the product and process of the children's programming by means of the visibility of trials, tests, errors and variations can offer opportunities for learning. And not only for the children who created the programme but also for the other children involved. Such software can thus become, through metacognitive processes, knowledge that can be re-applied and re-used (CRE, 2000a).

Formalising the behaviour of a robot by means of rules has important cognitive and metacognitive implications. On the one hand, the rule reifies the cause-effect relationship and supplies the children with an important linguistic instrument to talk about and reflect on reactive behaviours ('If the temperature increases then the robot turns on the fan'). On the other hand, the immediacy of interpretation and the readability of the rules allow the children to revisit their problem solving approaches ('... then we added this rule to teach the robot to turn on the fan when it's hot ...'). This is especially useful when their programs do not produce the expected results. Typically, children prefigure a wide and articulate context, with many actors involved, where their fantasies shape up and evolve. Therefore, a project needs ways of supporting the memory of the work done, both for documentation purposes and as a representation of the history of the programming and building choices. Moreover, the environment assumes a social context of use that is articulated on three roles: children, teachers, experts:

- The *children* collaborate among themselves and with teachers in all phases of the project, from the identification of the problem to the invention of a solution. They discuss and compare possible alternatives, inspect examples and modify them to suit their needs; they explore the potential and the limits of the technology; they are engaged in an iterative process of socially shared construction in which the hypotheses that emerge are subject to the judgment of the group and to empirical verification.

- The *teachers* mediate between children and technology to smooth the interaction and support the children's creativity and motivation. Some of the options of the programming environment enable teachers to configure it for specific project requirements. They can change the icons and names of the objects (actions, conditions, behaviours) and tune the parameters of actions (e.g., the scale factors of commands such as: forward; wait, etc.) and conditions (the thresholds of sensors).

- The *experts* can extend the environment adding the definition of new construction types, actions and conditions.

Case studies

The project field-testing covered two school years and involved three infant schools of the Reggio Emilia Municipality and three elementary schools in Sweden. For an in-depth description we refer to the final reports of CAB's educational partners (CRE, 2001; Gustafsson and Lindh, 2001). Here, our objective was to focus on how the research in the classroom had influenced the design of a programming environment usable by five-year-old children. So we limit our case studies only to projects in the Reggio infant schools. The following three projects show that:

- there are no cognitive obstacles to children programming cybernetic creatures;
- in the presence of a well defined context and specialised tools, children are capable of programming a robot;

- to support children's projects the complexity of the programming environment must be managed to provide powerful, specific primitives;
- the proposed environment was usable thanks to its appeal, the appropriate nature of its granularity, inspectability, and suitability for being an object of discussion and reflection.

RoboSports

A group of children in the La Villetta infant school experimented with the RoboSports kit. This system was especially developed for visitors to LEGO-LAND Parks and allows them quickly to participate in a robot contest. This kit comprises a playing field for two teams to compete in making a vehicle that carries as many balls as possible in a hole. The field is a table with two tracks, each composed of one black line and one back-lighted hole. The mechanical components are specialised, thus allowing the construction of a limited set of vehicles capable of transporting and pushing the balls into the hole. The software environment supplies primitives such as: a 'follow-the-line' behaviour, a condition that can be used to stop it when the light sensor detects a back-light, and translation and rotation commands to push the balls in the hole. The kit comes with video tutorials to help the users build and program the vehicles. At La Villetta school parents and teachers have built the playing field and the children have set up and programmed their vehicles for the contest.

This experience demonstrated that the children succeed in using the features of the programming environment to solve the problem, because the specialisation of the components simplified the construction of a vehicle suited to the task, and the visual programming environment that supplies only a limited, but powerful, set of primitives enabled the children to compose the program autonomously. Moreover, when engaged in group discussions to overcome programming errors, they spoke in terms of the icons of the programming language to annotate the playing field, as a symbolic representation of the program execution, when discussing the effects of the instructions given to their robots (CRE, 2000b). RoboSports is a good example of the potential a context-oriented system has. Its limit comes from being too specialised: the hardware and software components can only be used for this contest, or contests of this type, thus limiting the children's creativity.

Cybernetic adventures

The widespread interest shown in monsters by a class of children in the Neruda school over several years provoked the idea of constructing a scenario where the different identities of single cybernetic subjects and the characteristics of the context would allow the creation of a 'possible life'. This life would develop and evolve according to the frequency and quality of relations between the 'actors' (monsters or defenders of the city) (Barchi *et al,* 2001).

The monsters attacked a city; the inhabitants constructed walls and traps to defend themselves and organised a team of defenders to hold back the monsters. The monsters and the defenders had been constructed with defined behaviours that reflected the dynamics of a battle whose evolution and outcomes are unpredictable. Each monster was equipped with two touch sensors used to avoid obstacles and a light sensor pointing to the floor, to stop the vehicle if it entered a coloured zone. The monsters had a light mounted on the back that made them recognisable by the defenders, and a light sensor allowing them to move in the direction of the attack.

This first definition of the behaviours was such that, after colliding, the monsters and the defenders wandered over the playing field without a clear objective. A monster accidentally ended in the trap or succeeded in entering in the city; the defenders rambled without a clear strategy for blocking the monsters they encountered. The children recognised these limits and proposed alternatives, but the teachers could not implement the proposed mechanisms of attraction between the defenders and the monsters, and between the monsters and the city. So the experts were called in. They proposed two modifications to the project: to introduce tracks of a different colour showing the monster the direction to arrive at the city doors, and a modification of the program of the defenders, activating a mechanism for seeking the monster (i.e., turning around and detecting the direction of light). These proposals were discussed with the children, who modified the scenario and the robots so as to obtain the desired behaviours.

This project work has covered a long period over several phases: designing and realising the scenario, programming and experimentation, modifying the behaviours. By participating as design experts, the authors of this chapter ascertained the following:

- it is possible to capture the complexity of projects of this type in the proposed model

- complex behaviours such as those exemplified by this project cannot be developed by children on their own, but they *can* become part of a repertoire of specialised components that children can evaluate and apply.

This style of interaction with cybernetic objects can be defined as 'playing the psychologist' (Ackermann, 1991). 'Playing the psychologist' and 'playing the engineer' constitute the two ends of the spectrum of possible roles that children can adopt when they interact with a cybernetic construction kit. In the former, children observe and ask themselves questions on the nature of the object at hand (its intentions, 'intelligence', etc.), so as to understand its intimate nature; in the latter the construction and modification activities of the objects and their behaviours prevail. The children keep oscillating from one to the other, and the psychologist and engineer components are calibrated and arranged as various degrees of breakdown occur.

Giving other life

This project originated in the 1999/2000 school year at the Villetta infant school:

> ....from a group of five and six-year-old children who wished to help a large branch that had broken off from a tree due to a heavy snowfall. The children were well aware that they could create 'another kind of life' for the plant, which had now been sheltered in the school piazza. The children placed the digital tools and materials in relation with the sensors and actuators which they thought were most suited to allow the different subjects to communicate, and with other languages and materials (paper, wire, clay, structures built with recycled materials, etc.) that are a common feature of school life. The children's narration was the bond that held together the different levels at which the research was being conducted, constructing meanings, even provisional ones, and identifying new questions to be investigated'. (CRE, 2000b)

The following year (2000/2001), another group of 5 and 6-year-old children extended the project by adding a dialogue between a bird on the tree and its robot friend. During winter food supplies are scarce. The bird asks for the help of robot baker-boy that will bring crumbs to the tree. Once there, the robot will notify its friend, who will come down for the bread.

Because of growing up in a school where cybernetic constructions were just one of the things on offer, the second group of children found it natural to construct their robots and program them with the visual environment previously described. Here is how they summarised their understanding at the end of the project:

> 'Now we're real robot programmers!'
>
> 'It's true! This is a school of programmers! We can do all sorts of things!'
>
> 'We discovered three secrets:
>
> 1) two pieces of the measuring stick make one tile
>
> 2) if the bird touches the bend sensor, the recorder goes 'cheep, cheep'
>
> 3) robots can talk to each other with the envelope and the letter box.'
> (CRE, 2001)

The children solved a number of sub-tasks generated by the evolution of their work. One was to determine the value for the 'forward' command to let the robot move six tiles on the floor. To this end the children built a measuring stick, mark-

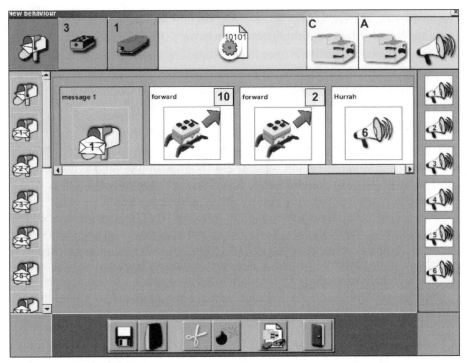

Figure 30

ing the distance travelled for various values of the parameter for the 'forward' command. Experimenting with these values they discovered that 'two pieces of the measuring stick make one tile' and 'forward 12' was the solution to their problem (see Fig. 30). The magic number of 'two pieces' did not come by accident. The programmable brick controls the amount of time the motors are on; how this time correlates to the distance travelled is a function of the actual vehicle details (tires, gears, weight, terrain, etc.). The software allows specifying a scale factor to tune the result, and the teachers customised it for this project.

Motivated children can work hard at exploring various courses of action. They also show greater competence than one tends to attribute to children of this age. The software should enable children to pursue their experiments by narrowing the gap between the robot primitives and the children's viewpoint. If the interface were to use time measures to represent units of movement, this would make the command less readable: one would need to translate between time and distance. By leaving only a number and providing customisation via a 'hidden' scale factor, we make room for the interpretation that the input to 'forward' is some unit of space. The children followed this interpretation and set up an experiment to discover the robot's unit of distance. Making 'forward 2' correspond to a tile on a floor allowed the children to be in control of the process.

The children built their robots in such a way that they could tell the story of the bird and his friend while the robots were playing it out. Synchronisation points are essential to a good result. The robot should start moving when the bird calls it. An initial solution was to use a sound sensor to hear the voice of the bird (see secret no. 2). Unfortunately a sound sensor picks up noise and does not understand language. So any noise was good enough to trigger the robot behaviour. By inspecting the software interface the children noticed the message icons, tried them out and discovered that robots 'can talk to each other with the envelope and the letter box'. Exchanging messages provided a robust mechanism for synchronisation, thus enabling the children to complete their project (see Fig. 30).

In the upper left corner three sensors are shown: the message receiver (active), and a sound and a light sensor that are left over from previous design approaches. To move forward 12, the children used two commands (10 + 2) as the interface provides a slider (not shown in Figure) that limits the parameter values to the range (0 .. 10).

The software interface does attempt to reveal what is possible with the programmable brick, by organising the available features into boxes that contain components of the same type (Fig. 28a). Furthermore, the structure of boxes reflects a concrete vs. virtual distinction: tangible sensors and actuators, built-in devices (i.e., sound and messages, that are not associated to a pluggable hardware component) and virtual devices (i.e., those implemented via software: timers, counters). This taxonomy is reflected into the operational structure of the interface that supports children while exploring, discovering and learning the available features.

Conclusions

We based our work on the notion of a competent child who can pursue difficult projects for extended periods of time in a supportive learning environment. We assumed that children would be interested in building their own animated constructions and programming their behaviours. The CAB project has shown that, in a supportive learning environment, children can and will design and build animated construction behaviours. We have proposed and prototyped a visual programming language that is not general purpose but rather strives for simplicity and power by incorporating knowledge of the construction types and the specificity of the project at hand.

A cybernetic construction kit endowed with a tangible programming interface, and redesigned to improve its mechanical system and the readability of active components, should enable children to explore the material freely and autonomously (without the need for external 'experts') while engaging in motivating projects.

Acknowledgments

This work has greatly benefited from continuous interaction with all the partners of the CAB project. We wish to thank all the adults and children that have accepted the challenge to use and experiment with the LEGO kit and our prototypes; the work described here could have not been done without their enthusiasm, creative input and support. The prototypes developed for the CAB project and cited in this paper do not imply any commitment from the LEGO company to incorporate them in future products.

Chapter Seven

Caress – 'an endearing touch'

Phil Ellis
University of Sunderland

his definition of the project acronym from *Chambers 20th Century Dictionary* provides both the grounding and the background to the CARESS project. The approach to music in mainstream education which I developed during the 1970s and 80s (Ellis, 1987) put children at the centre of activity, giving them responsibility for their learning. Central to this was a focus on creativity, communication and expression, primarily in the medium of sound, and the technology was the tool for everyone to realise their imaginative ideas.

Since 1992 I have been researching in special schools, mainly with children who have profound and multiple learning difficulties (PMLD). These children are often have no self-help skills whatsoever and may have impaired muscular control, speech, sight and hearing. Accordingly, I have developed a therapy, called Sound Therapy, which puts children at the centre of the activity. By being immersed in a sound environment can often help them to develop control, expression and communication skills (Ellis, 1994, 1997). This on-going research (*Incidental Music*, Ellis, 1996a), gives strong focus to sound, and it was this research that led to the CARESS project.

The i[3] call provided the perfect opportunity to develop aspects of this philosophy of learner-centred approaches. The i[3] Experimental School Environments specifically called for 'open and visionary approaches' to learning. Moreover it encouraged a move away from the 'linear pattern of 'user requirements' ... (to) a non-linear and iterative mixing of activities such as 'generation of concepts', 'development of mock-ups', 'understanding learners', 'creation of prototypes', 'evaluation' and 'technological research', 'refinement of concepts' ' – all of which chimed beautifully with the *Incidental Music* project. Even more resonant was the i[3] special focus on the development of IT tools 'that encourage and enhance discovery, creativity, thinking and expression'.

In my work with PMLD children I have observed how these children, who normally have very limited control over their own bodies and next to no control over their environment, gradually become more functional and self-aware as they are able to control their sound environment, even through the most minimal of head movements. The term '*Aesthetic Resonation*' was coined to describe the special moments when a child achieves real control and expression after a period of intense exploration, discovery and creation – moments which can be seen to be both 'endearing' and 'touching'!. Enjoyment and self-motivation are key aspects of this approach (Izard, 1971; Maslow, 1970; Koestler, 1979). It is readily transferable to mainstream education and also responsive to the provision and evaluation of new devices that interact with the various senses.

Central to Sound Therapy is a piece of technology called a Soundbeam. Invented by Edward Williams, a Bristol-based composer in England, this device was initially conceived to allow dancers to create their own music through their physical movements. To date, its greatest impact has been with the disabled, as even the smallest physical movement can enable expressive control of, and interaction with, sound. Sound remains relatively unexplored as a means of motivation, communication and expression when compared to our predominantly visually-based culture. In spite of a burgeoning commercial music 'industry', placing sound as the true primary experience is a rare phenomenon. The Soundbeam works by emitting an ultrasonic beam of sound from a sensor. A movement within this beam results in the Soundbeam controller generating MIDI code, which in turn generates sound. There is no problem of latency, because as the sound generation is coincident with the physical movement, it generates a feeling of absolute and immediate interactive control. This system is at the heart of Sound Therapy.

In Sound Therapy an environment is created in which the child is placed at the centre, and empowered through a developing ability to take control of their environment and activity. Small physical movements can produce the means of developing expression with sound. Over time this can lead to the development of self awareness, self confidence and self-esteem. Being in this environment may often be the only time in their lives when they have any control of what happens. The project acronym was coined from this work: **C**reating **A**esthetically **R**esonant **E**nvironment**S** in **S**ound.

Project Summary
The purpose of CARESS was to enable young children to learn and develop physical and cognitive skills by interacting with a responsive sound environment. The combination of a sensor and a sensor-to-sound interface provided the means

for exploring expressive interaction and creativity with sound, within a controlled sonic environment.

Advances in movement sensors and other technology have utilised various electronic media to create human-machine interfaces with apparently significant, but largely unexplored, educational potential. Such systems have often been developed for purposes outside the sphere of formal school education (e.g. performance art, dance, VR environments, video animation and medical applications), yet preliminary research demonstrates that it is the school environment in which such technology could contribute most dramatically, particular with young children. The *Incidental Music* project research into the educational experience of young children with PMLD, who had missed out on early learning and for whom the first experience of enjoyable control and initiation has evidently been a crucial educational motivator, demonstrated the potential with young children in both special needs and mainstream education.

Partners

The CARESS partners comprised Phil Ellis (co-ordinator) and Lisa Percy, originally based at the Institute of Education, University of Warwick, but based in the School of Arts, Design, Media and Culture at the University of Sunderland. for the final months of the project The main focus of their work was to explore possibilities for Sound Therapy through the use of new sensors and developing the associated learning paradigm. They also conducted a pilot study applying the method and technologies in a mainstream school. Through development of curriculum materials for mainstream children aged 4-8, we could make observations to test the effectiveness of the technology in this domain and see what the possibilities were for the new sensors developed in the project.

Working in parallel as a therapeutic educator was Stefan Hasselblad at Emaljskolan in Sweden, who had experience of using the Soundbeam for his work with children who had special needs. His application allowed the methodology itself to be assessed and improved in terms of its transferability and then documented for teachers and therapists. The materials developed in England were trialled in the Swedish environment to test for effectiveness and relevance.

The third partner was based in the Department of Electrical and Electronic Engineering, University of Bristol. Dr Nishan Canagarajah, assisted by Dr Paul Masri, were active in research into medical and digital music synthesis. Their role was to provide new sensors as well as hardware and software technology support.

Further invaluable support was provided by the Soundbeam Project, Bristol UK, who manufacture and market the Soundbeam equipment which was at the heart of the CARESS project. They actively supported the project in terms of access to new equipment and know how and in looking at the potential for Soundbeam as a creative tool in mainstream schools.

Early Learning

In summary, the aims of CARESS were:

- to expand the Sound Therapy research by introducing various new devices and interfaces interacting with the senses, using the children with special needs in the UK and Sweden and the proven methodology to evaluate and improve their design.
- to extend the use of these cognitive tools into mainstream education via pilot studies with groups of 4-8 year olds in mainstream schools, modifying the new devices to accommodate the different expectations of these children.
- to use the Swedish and UK experiences to assess and develop a transferable methodology and so evolve accessible written, video and other resources for teachers to use, promoting the development of this new model of learning both in special education and mainstream arts education

If we can be immersed within sound itself, we eventually generate the space and stillness to explore, to resonate, and to develop our own creativity most directly. By shifting the focus away from external (intrusive) to internal (non-intrusive) motivation, by working in an environment where the focus is predominantly on sound, and by placing the child at the centre of activity, much unexpected development and progression has been observed in children with special needs (Ellis and Laufer, 2000). The benefits of providing these opportunities to young children in mainstream education are likely to be different but no less profound. Working in 'sound – expressive' ways resonates with Koestler's investigations in the area of creativity and mathematics which have highlighted an area where non-verbal thinking seems to predominate and where, as Koestler (1989) observed: 'we have to get away from speech to think clearly'.

The requirements for creativity are generally agreed to have three components, described by the mathematician Huntley as: *surprise*, at an unexpected encounter; *curiosity*, wanting to know why; *wonder*, that we have chanced on an unexplored world that appears boundless. (Huntley, 1970). Sound Therapy builds upon these foundations and develops skills of general applicability so that severely handicapped children can:

- perform, communicate, listen and compose with sound
- often show 'aesthetic resonance' by their facial expressions
- are actively involved for extended periods of time

- reveal an ability for concentration not apparent elsewhere
- begin to discover, explore, give expression to and communicate their own feelings
- make significant physical responses – movements and gestures not seen before, or not previously made independently

By introducing new sensors and actuators we hoped to make it easier to tailor the equipment configuration to suit the needs of the individual. For example, for a child who has severely limited ability to move and significant muscle wastage, an EMG 'muscle sensor' can detect the nerve activity of their intention to move and use this to trigger and control the sound. This was intended to be used as a precursor to the Soundbeam, which requires the capacity for visible movement. Though developed for disabled children, such sensors are readily available and applicable to young children in mainstream education. This is why we decided to iterate on the development of new devices for disabled children and the proven methodologies developed in Sound Therapy, and to repeat similar iterative trials of the developed devices with young children in the mainstream sector, where we expected different kinds of feedback. For example, we suspected that the mainstream children might seek to control several sensors at once. One child might simultaneously control several sound properties through different sensors, thereby learning more complex interactions and improving their dexterity. We were especially keen to see groups of children co-operating in defining the sound evolution. We had already observed signs of shared activity with certain disabled children who seldom communicated so we were interested in the potential development of shared activity.

New Tools

Preliminary discussions between the three partners produced several ideas for new portable and wearable devices that interact with the senses and complement the original Soundbeam. These provided our initial starting point of ideas for new devices on which to iterate:

- Electromyographic (EMG) 'muscle' sensor
- Optical Fibre Goniometers (OFG) 'joint angle' sensor
- Soundbox, Soundchair and Soundbed vibro-tactile resonators
- Soundbeam movement sensor system
- Intuitive sound palette
- Video gesture recognition system

The EMG and OFG sensors were developments and they provided the main focus for technological development.

Electromyographic (EMG) 'muscle' sensor

Two types of sensors had been developed at Bristol University for medical application, where they were combined with a muscle stimulator to achieve closed-loop feedback for Functional Electrical Stimulation. The Electromyographic (EMG) sensor uses a pair of closely spaced electrical pads (fingertip size) to pick up muscular activity when placed on the skin over a muscle. As the muscle contracts, the signal activity increases, though not in linear relation. In Sound Therapy applications control is more important than the exact profile. The sensitivity of the EMG sensors is such that they have been used to detect the intention to activate a muscle, even for people who cannot engage a muscular contraction. As long as the neural pathways and nerves are functional, signals can be detected. So these sensors can be musically enabling for able-bodied and disabled children alike.

Optical Fibre Goniometer (OFG) 'angle' sensor

An Optical Fibre Goniometer (OFG) determines the angle across a joint. It is essentially a small length of optical fibre that has been treated to condition the amount of transmission loss under bending. The ends of the sensor are attached to the body, either side of a joint. One end of the fibre is illuminated and at other end there is a detector. Flexing the joint bends the sensor and produces a measurable change in the light received at the detector. This function too is not linear and can suffer a little hysteresis, but this is of no consequence since the goal is functional control not accurate measurement. Between them, these two wearable sensors can detect a reasonable amount of body movement. The fact that they are wearable was exploited by developing a pocket-sized wireless interface box, leaving the wearer free to move in space with no trailing wires. This latter development was seen to be particularly useful in mainstream schools where children are generally mobile.

Given the intended users of this technology, the key design criteria were robustness, ease of use (e.g. automatic calibration), being compact and light, cost-effectiveness, and ease of manufacture.

Soundbeam Movement Sensor System

Leon Theremin was the first to develop the idea of a musical instrument which could be played without any physical contact (Glinsky, 2000). His invention was the inspiration behind Soundbeam, but beyond the touch-free interface the mechanisms are dissimilar. The Soundbeam combines an ultrasound transmitter and receiver, calibrated to measure distance in discrete steps. Originally designed for dancers, it incorporates a variable ranging control which allows its active zone to be compressed into a few centimetres or stretched out to cover a wide area. In practice this means that the invisible instrument can be varied in size to accommodate the movements the player wishes to perform or is capable of performing. Soundbeam has its own integrated sensor-to-sound interface that translates information about the speed and direction of movement of the closest object in its path into MIDI control codes. The MIDI (Musical Instrument Digital Interface) is the standard control port on synthesisers.

Because the CARESS project only ran for eighteen months we focused mainly on these three devices, but the CARESS website provides information about the more intuitive sound palette.

Educational Evaluation

Layered Analysis was developed as a qualitative research tool for the evaluation of Sound Therapy (Ellis, 1996b). This methodology was used in CARESS to assess the effectiveness of the new tools and devices in developing the initial design of each device with disabled children and then refining it with young children in mainstream schools. In special education this methodology involves using the video recordings made of every session, disassembling and reassembling them to build up a comprehensive and detailed series of pictures of each individual.

Layered Analysis was used in England and Sweden, and the video materials thus produced significantly enhanced the interaction and exchange of results between Sweden and the UK.

The video processing is in five stages:

1. *Source tape*: The complete, original recording of each session. This is not kept from week to week but provides a full record of each session. Its function is the temporary storage of data, allowing relevant sequences and events to be identified and archived.

2. *Master tape*: Significant examples of behaviour during a session are identified and copied from the source tape. The master tape recording thus gradually increases in length from week-to-week. This provides a detailed, chronological account of behaviour from every session.

3. *Layers tape*: Particular responses are selected and recorded separately. For example, each time a child uses his right arm, or plays a particularly stimulating sound, might form one layer of information. For each child there may be six or seven discrete layers of information providing a detailed series of sequences revealing particular patterns of behaviour, development and progression.

4. *Snapshots tape*: One significant example from every month of the pro-gramme is chosen from the master tape. These examples are recorded sequentially to provide a highly compressed chronological sequence of development. This provides brief but precise details of their progress and performance for teachers and parents.

5. *Summary tape*: Limited to ten or fifteen minutes for each individual, this provides a visual summary of a child's development from the start of the pro-gramme, but may not include examples from every month. Where an individual has been involved in Sound Therapy for many months or several years this tape is illustrative of their development and is useful in situations where time is at a premium.

In day-to-day classroom situations it is easier to monitor progression and development formatively by looking only at the source tape and/or making notes during sessions. Layered Analysis was an essential feature of the research associated with this project, but is clearly inappropriate for day-to-day teacher assessment.

Iteration between Partners
The new device ideas were fed into the project in the first twelve months or so of the project. Each was evaluated and refined in a special needs environment, then further refined by use and observation in the mainstream schools. The partners met regularly every three months to discuss developments.

Achievements
1. Technology
From the technical viewpoint, this project aimed to assist the educational partners by producing portable, wearable and sharable technology, so the objectives of Sound Therapy could be extended within special needs education and extended to mainstream primary education. Two wearable sensors were chosen to complement the existing spatial sensor that is part of the Soundbeam system and a wireless link was proposed to give greater freedom of movement to wearers, particularly those in mainstream education.

The proposed muscle sensor was rapidly developed and delivered to the educational partners. At the initial project meeting, it was decided that the angle sensor should be integrated with the wireless link because of its greater applicability to the more mobile mainstream school environment. The sensor was also developed quickly, but there were problems in designing the wireless links to the specifications proposed. Efforts to produce the design quickly (for rapid iteration between partners) conflicted with the aims to make it small and low power, since power and space optimisations take time and often several iterations of prototypes. A trade-off was made, which compromised the robustness of the channel and resulted in more time being spent on troubleshooting than we might have wished.

We had not foreseen one element of design: the fabrics used to make the sensors wearable. In order to fit well and orient the sensors correctly to the body, we had to go through a few iterations of fabric design for each sensor. And there was also inadequate provision in the proposal for the production of the units. With custom mechanical parts, surface mount electronic components and tight interconnections, building, assembly and testing were challenging and time consuming. All in all, prototype production and fabric design for the ten muscle sensors and the four wireless bend sensors took roughly six person months.

The technology was developed in an iterative manner, in collaboration with the educational partners. This was challenging for the technical partner who had to turn around designs as quickly as possible; the educational partners had to work with prototype equipment in real educational environments, and all concerned had to develop a common language for effective communication of feedback.

Experiences with the bend sensor showed that optical fibres are not ideal materials to subject to regular severe bending stresses – but this does not mean that bend sensors should be abandoned as a wearable technology. For future projects, we need to define sensor *applications* rather than specific sensors at the proposal stage, so freeing us to explore a variety of simple and easily manufactured technologies, to aid the rapid prototyping. The simplicity, flexibility and power of software-based synthesis enabled rapid creation of a number of distinct sound environments. In combination with movement sensors, they can catalyse the creativity of participants to be expressive. Further exploration in this area is needed, ideally with real-time collaboration with educational researchers and direct input from participants into the design process.

2. Mainstream Curriculum Materials

A number of classroom projects were developed and tried out. Designed to fit with the English National Curriculum requirements, they were applicable to both mainstream and special needs (ADHD) environments. They were subsequently trialed in Swedish schools. Some of these are briefly described below.

Dreamscapes
Objectives:
This is a cross-curricular activity which enables a group to create a performance piece. It draws on the dance, music, English and art curricula.

Figure 31: Dream sequence

Aim of the game:

Using sound and gesture as expressive media, the group created a dream sequence of their own design (See fig. 31).

A performance was constructed based upon the theme of dreams. During rehearsals the children selected sounds and explored their qualities. They then developed a movement sequence which expressed their own dream stories.

The children were encouraged to focus upon the ways in which sound and movement enabled interaction within the group. They decided that the performance should be in three sections, each exploring a different kind of dream.

With the help of props and basic costumes, they ultimately performed their dance. Using both the Soundbeam and EMG sensors enabled them to express a range of movements and effects.

Roamer
Objectives:

To develop skills in control programming.
To listen for and identify different sounds and pitches.

Aim of the game:

To program the roamer to play the beam in different ways. Initially this should be to make one high sound, one low sound and a mid-pitch sound.

The roamer (See Fig.32) is a programmable device the children can manipulate in order to play the Soundbeam. This game encourages children to listen for and identify different pitches and to develop their programming skills.

Once they have programmed the roamer to play along the length of the beam in order to investigate the notes available, the group can move on to the next stage. They have to programme the roamer to play one high, one low sound and one mid-pitch sound.

Once this basic level has been mastered, the teacher is free to explore the potential for designing programmable routes for creating a composition, as the roamer passes through and pauses at chosen points along the beam. This in turn can be extended to develop a link with storytelling activities, as the roamer visits certain points in the narrative and/or activates sound as each scene takes place.

Navigator
Objectives:

To improve listening skills and spatial awareness. To learn the points of the compass. To understand fractions and degrees of a turn.

Figure 32: The Roamer

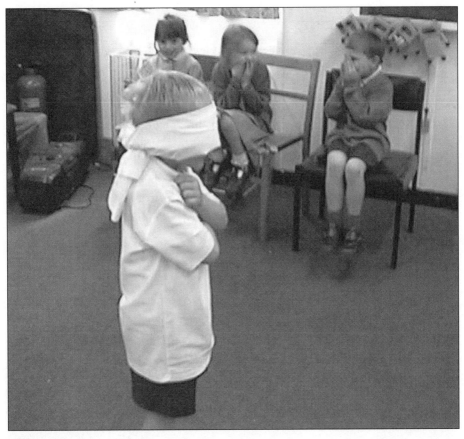

Figure 33: Locating the Sound

Aim of the game:

To navigate around the space using only sound as a guide and, where appropriate, spoken directions. The player wears a blindfold (See Fig. 33) and the task is to locate the source of the sound (the Soundbeam sensor).

The chief objectives of this game are to develop listening skills, recognition of pitch and spatial awareness. Wearing a blindfold, the player is required to find the sound and navigate to the highest note.

Depending upon the teacher's objectives, the number of players and the skills of the children, further developments can be made. As the player navigates the space, others can give instructions using left/right/forward/back, compass points, and fractions or degrees of a turn.

Stepping Stones
Objectives:

To develop motor control and listening skills. To enhance reaction times and physical co-ordination.

Aim of the game:

The player should work his/her way along the length of the beam. When an 'active' part of the beam is reached sound will be heard. The player should aim to stand as still as possible. When they have achieved silence they should walk along the beam until the next sound is activated and then immediately freeze for the duration of the sound (See Fig 34). If the player wobbles or moves this will reactivate sound and silence will not be achieved.

This game was developed as an extension to Navigator. The Soundbeam is set so that four different notes can be played along its length. Each of these notes will sound for 4 seconds once activated. There is a space between each note. The child is then asked to find the first note on the beam. As soon as the sound is heard the

Figure 34: Walking along the Soundbeam

child must become as still as possible, so as not to re-trigger the sound. Once the sound has expired the child moves forward and steps into the next sound. Again, they must remain still until silence is achieved.

Stepping Stones focuses upon the development of physical control and listening skills. It provides a useful exercise for children who have difficulty keeping still. It can be played as a stand alone activity or used as the introduction to a lesson requiring good listening skills and/or quick physical responses.

Speed
Objectives:
To explore the concepts of volume and speed. To improve the control and understanding of gesture as a means of expression.

To improve physical control, interaction, listening skills and an understanding of volume and expressive physical movement.

Aim of the game:
To work alone, in pairs or groups to control sound through speed of gesture and produce an expressive piece of movement and sound.

Speed enables players to explore the relationship between sound and gesture afforded by sensor technology (See Fig. 35). The faster the player moves in the Soundbeam the louder the sound produced.

This activity can be played in several ways. One player can be asked to move along the length of the beam making the least possible sound. Once they have reached the highest note they can turn and move quickly back to their starting point, creating the maximum volume. This enhances an awareness of physical speed and encourages control through the powerful link with sound. This activity is particularly useful for those who have difficulties in maintaining physical control.

Figure 35: Exploring the relationship between sound and gesture

Two players can engage in a dialogue of gesture and sound, each interpreting the movement of the other and responding to it in an aesthetic context. In order to develop observational skills as well as interactivity, one player can try to mimic the movements and sounds created by the other.

Throw and Catch
Objectives:
To develop and practice skills of sending and receiving in response to an aural stimulus.
This game will develop hand – eye co-ordination skills and listening skills.
It encourages anticipation, concentration and develops good reaction times.

Aim of the game:
To throw and catch a ball with another player (See fig. 36). The ball may not be thrown until the beam produces no sound. The game should be played as fast as possible.

As the ball passes between the two players, the Soundbeam is activated. At the simplest level the players should catch the ball, wait for silence and then return it. The 'gate' time of the sound can be altered to suit the players. A longer gate time would suit beginners whereas older children may be able to cope with a faster pace.

Figure 36: Caught 'on the quiet'

The basic game can be extended to a team activity and the focus adjusted to suit the skill and ability of the players. For example, a child may have to perform an activity such as placing the ball at his/her feet, or running to touch the wall, before the sound ceases. A different aim may be to keep a continuous sound, or to race with another team.

Evaluation

The games which used only Soundbeam technology (Throw and Catch, Roamer, Speed, Navigator, Stepping Stones) clearly revealed the success of transferring aspects of the Sound Therapy approach from special needs to mainstream schools. The sensor technology showed the potential to enhance expressive gesture and could be additionally developed and refined so as to take this enhancement much further.

Making a physical and cognitive link between physical gesture as simultaneous with expression in sound has introduced sound as a valuable addition to a range of curriculum areas including art, writing, dance, drama and music and to imaginative and expressive domains. In a child-centred educational environment the developments have enhanced the opportunities for children to take control of their learning. They have used the direct control they have between sound and movement to develop their creative work both individually and collaboratively.

At the ages of 4-8, which were the focus of this project, children are developing rapidly in many areas, particularly motor control, spatial awareness, interactivity, listening skills, reaction times, collaboration and expressive potential. The CARESS project has shown that in all these areas using technology for aesthetic experience has made a contribution to development. It has allowed the children to work in ways which would otherwise have been impossible, so it has enriched the primary curriculum experience for children whose abilities vary widely.

Special Needs

We found both in Sweden and England that children's mobility, awakening grade, facial and vocal expression, body awareness and joy increased because of the CARESS project. They were also able to have more control over their environment through sound. The children with severe ADHD related problems gained self-esteem, motor control, taking instruction, concentration and diminution of involuntary movements. They participated with great joy and possibly the best motivation considering their school situation. Mostly they have worked with different variations of the Throw and Catch games. The EMG sensor showed valuable potential for the children with special needs, although further refinement was needed to adjust and control the sensitivity and make its performance entirely predictable.

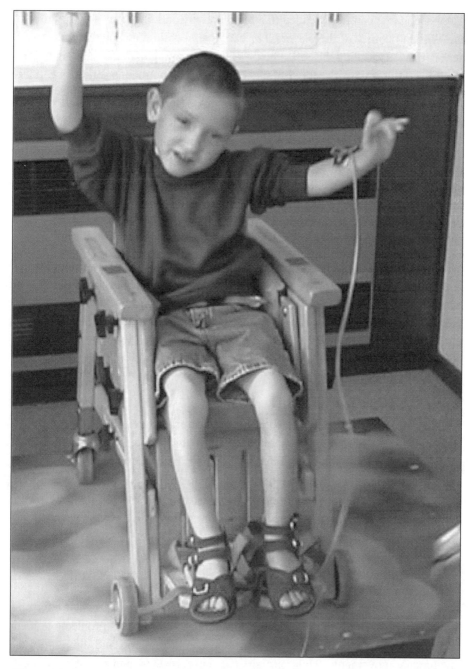

Figure 37: 'Lenny' expressing himself

That the EMG was not wireless produced problems for mobility, even for children who were wheelchair users and had little independent movement. Similarly there was the issue of intrusiveness. Fixing the EMG to the skin reminded some children of plasters and some found it painful to remove the device at the end of a session. The OFG, although wireless, was rather bulky and heavy, and its rather limited field of operation did not appear to support creative exploration and expression. These issues were explored in the Kidslab workshop run for CARESS (see Kidslab and CARESS below).

The one shining example of these new sensors' potential was illustrated by the experience of a 7 year old boy. Lenny had cerebral palsy. He was able to communicate effectively even though his level of development was below average. Before commencing Sound Therapy, he was reluctant to use the left side of his body, in particular his left arm. He had worked on a programme of physiotherapy which focused on his arm movements, but this had not noticeably increased when we started working with him. Before Sound Therapy Lenny seemed to lack the motivation to exercise his limbs and trunk. He was reluctant to stretch and would not use his left arm. He would sometimes become distressed during physiotherapy sessions, complaining of discomfort and tiredness, and needed much encouragement in order to complete his exercises.

Almost from the first session in Sound Therapy Lenny became animated, smiled, and showed pleasure in physical action. We placed the EMG on his left forearm (see Fig.37), and although we did not ask him to move, he spontaneously and with evident enjoyment used both arms to control sound to achieve expression.

Lenny clearly enjoyed the experience of Sound Therapy and showed considerable physical progression. The dramatic increase in his use of his left arm is directly attributed by the school staff to his experience in these sessions. It is pleasing that these physical developments have transferred into his daily life. Working with sound as an expressive medium, over which he had total control, has clearly been motivational. Lenny chose to exercise his limbs and trunk during the sessions, whereas he was reluctant to move in this way in physiotherapy. As his confidence grew, he became more flexible, making larger reaches and bends of the body. He also showed the ability to make fine movements in order to create a particular effect, revealing an improved awareness and control of his hands and fingers.

It seems clear that for Lenny the potential for additional sensors, plus the non-intrusive, internal motivation provided by the Sound Therapy approach was a powerful and effective combination.

Sensor	Measurement	Functional requirements	Attaching to the body	User requirements	Research issues	Costs (Note 1)
EMG	Muscle activity	Measure movement	Anywhere (over relevant muscle)	Easy to attach to body. Lightweight.	Electrode materials/ contact paste. Electrical safety	30 euro
Optical Fiber	Angle/direction	Measure bending	joints	Easy to attach to body. Lightweight.	Application to body. Range, sensitivity and accuracy	50 euro
Accelerometer	Velocity, speed, distance, direction. 1, 2 or 3D.	Measure movement	end of limb	Easy to attach to body. Lightweight.	Range, sensitivity, accuracy.Calibration and threshold effects	50 euro (3D movement)

Note 1: Cost is estimated for medium volume production (1000 units).

Table 2

Kidslab and CARESS

KidsLab organised a workshop on action-related sound in December 1999 at the University of Limerick in Ireland. Although this was close to the end of the CARESS project it proved stimulating, since many of the issues raised by the project were explored and discussed in depth and generated useful interchange of ideas.

Discussions centred around four fields of expertise involved in CARESS: sensor technology, sound design, learning and play, and mapping between sound and movement. Worthy of a chapter on their own, some of the most interesting results are summarised below.

Sensor Technology

A variety of sensors were explored with respect to:

- how and what they measure
- functional requirements
- the way they can be worn
- user requirements

All three alternatives above were 'wired', i.e. the user was constrained by wires in some way. If a wireless solution were implemented, this would make the issue of battery operation, and therefore battery life, a significant factor.

Sound Design

Issues here included how to create controllable sounds which are:

- interesting, useful and meaningful
- (re-)configurable (i.e. personalised)
- dynamic
- possible to sequence
- can be recorded and imported by children

Learning and Play

Teachers find current curricula in primary schools in England extremely task oriented. A balance is needed between cognitive and social-emotional development in schools. So new learning tools are desirable which focus on supporting the emergence of aesthetic motivation, the development of expressive and interactive skills and the expression and communication of emotions.

Educational environments are needed in which:

- children can create complex sound structures
- children can explore expressiveness through body movement

SENSOR- SOUND TECHNOLOGY CAN SUPPORT LEARNING AND PLAY CONCERNING

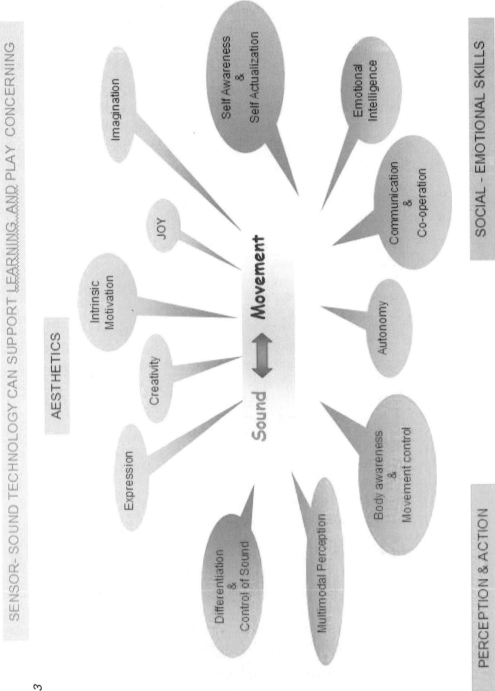

Table 3

Table 4

AREA	USER NEEDS	TECHNOLOGY REQUIREMENTS
SENSORS	• Unrestricted movement • Easy and stable attachable and detachable • measurements mirroring conscious movement changes	• Wireless/power issues • Material & shape for attachment, light weight sensors • sensor type which matches experience level
SOUND	• Wide range of sounds (instrumental, environmental, mechanical...) • Morphable sound	• Sound generation system allowing easy new input of recorded sound • From MIDI to Sonic Browsing
MOVEMENT-SOUND MAPPING	• Intuitive mapping adaptable to different perceptual-motor as well as task contexts	• Real-time sound processing • Sensitivity of sound and sensor input independently adaptable
LEARNING & PLAY	• Wide range of contexts • Intuitive use of the system • Good Instructions • Stable • Low costs	• Eventually different sensors • HCI • Instructions specific to contexts of use • Unbreakable & crash proof • Low material and production costs

Mapping between sound and movement

The workshop enabled the theme of inter-disciplinary working to be pursued, while offering the opportunity for sharing ideas with those from the same specialist background(s). Seeing at first hand the work of other researchers proved invaluable. The sensor technology being developed at the University of Limerick provided an interesting comparison with the CARESS interfaces being developed at Bristol, and sparked ideas for possible future research developments.

The focused discussion groups enabled researchers engaged in similar areas to share ideas and begin to unpack some of the theory behind current research contexts. The opportunity to involve students from the interactive design institute was welcome. The students shared their experience of design and educational work and were often able to present some of the questions project researchers take for granted once engaged with their research.

Above all, the two days enabled all participants to share their experiences with people from diverse backgrounds. With attendees engaged in education, electronics and the arts, a wealth of new ideas were open to discussion and exploration. It was a pity time ran out before concrete scenarios could be developed so everyone could gain a more tangible grasp of some of the concepts which had been introduced. The chance to spend time in 'soundboarding' and 'brainstorming' sessions is always welcomed, particularly among creative and imaginative colleagues in related disciplines, and the experience in the Limerick workshop had brought a greater focus to the current CARESS project as well as raising questions for new avenues and questions for investigation in future work.

Legacy

After CARESS ended, three new research projects based at the University of Sunderland are taking the ideas and techniques of Sound Therapy forward. Enabling non-specialist teachers and carers to exploit the techniques of the therapy with special needs children is being pursued in two special schools, involving children aged 6 to 16. One aim of Incidental Music was to develop an approach which did not require intense specialist training, either in teaching and learning methodologies or in the use of complex or unwieldy technology. It seems clear already that the technology itself and the learning techniques are readily accessible, even by self-confessed technophobes!

A second, three-year project is following up an earlier pilot study in work with the elderly in long-term care. We are working with elderly mentally infirm (EMI) who experience stroke, dementia and depression. This can be challenging and often very moving. The techniques and the technology explored in the CARESS project are proving effective in this domain and the next year of this project has the potential to make significant impact on the quality of life and experience for these people.

The aspect of expressive dance using the technology currently available is a focus of two courses being developed at the University of Sunderland. Some of the earlier foundation research done in movement with the primary school children in the CARESS project is being taken further, and again it is the children who are designing and discovering new ways forward, both for themselves as dancers, and through using the technology in different locations and contexts. This is suggesting new possibilities, including ideas for new types of sensor. Together with the exploitation of the emerging wireless technology, and the use of technology to give a more interactive and fluid access to sound, we are actively working towards new research proposals to capitalise on the possibilities being uncovered.

Although CARESS was a short-lived project we managed to fulfil its aims. We were fortunate that, as often happens in research, we created more questions than answers. These provide many avenues for further exploration and development, as well as on-going research and dissemination.

Chapter Eight

How children contribute to the design of technology for their own use

Lieselotte van Leeuwen
School of Arts, Design, Culture and Media
University of Sunderland, UK

Involving children in ESE projects

The projects presented in this book are unique in illustrating how children as co-designers can inform a design process. It is fascinating to compare the different approaches towards the same objective: using digital technology to make early education more engaging and stimulating. Thanks to the structure of the ESE initiative most projects brought together partners from academia, industry and school communities. The way children were involved reflects the multi-disciplinary character and shows the complexity of topics taken into account. Methods from academic research and design approaches were adapted and inter-related to meet the goals of each project. The children's input undoubtably provided crucial insights for the design teams. However, the question of how on one hand to give a voice to children, and determining the best ways of creating design relevant information on the other, is still far from resolved and requires further exploration.

This chapter offers an overview of the different ways children took part in the ESE projects and of the insights gained and topics to be addressed in this exciting new field of child-centered design methodology.

The children's involvement seems to be shaped by the choices the design teams made about:

- the relationship between technology and behaviour
- concepts of learning
- methods for involving children

The relationship between technology and behaviour

Although all the projects aimed to improve learning environments by means of technology, the starting points differed. Some projects chose a certain technology and subsequently analysed its potential for learning (Cab, KidStory, Playground). Others started with a concrete learning problem and then searched for or designed technology which could help solve it (NIMIS, CARESS). The difference in starting points is significant.

When starting with technology, the interaction with children will be focused around aspects of this technology. The design team first seeks to understand what kind of behaviour is supported by the given technology and how to change the design so as to improve the learning environment. A clear example is the use of KidPad software as a facilitator for linear and non linear storytelling in the KidStory project (see Stanton *et al* in this volume). The reaction of the children to this software determined what changes and additions should be made to the software and hardware. The outcome of this approach is a design-focused iterative process in which the children switch between being co-designers and users.

When projects start with the children's behaviour, the first concern is to try to understand the conditions under which certain behavioural patterns occur or fail to occur. The intention of the observer or facilitator is to gather behavioural information which allows us to specify technology out of a range of possibilities which might support specific forms of learning. As an example, the NIMIS project (see Cooper *et al* in this volume) started with a fine-tuned and complex analysis of classroom behaviour. It identified the needs of both children and teachers according to three pre-defined contexts: collaboration, literacy development and storytelling. The result was a list of pedagogical claims (Cooper *et al.,* 2000) from which classroom scenarios were developed and these provided the basis for the development and implementation of the software and hardware. What informed the design team was the interaction between children, teachers and technology in their everyday classroom context. While children weren't explicitly accorded the role of co-designers, they did strongly guide the design process in their role as pupils and later users of technology. This approach allowed outcomes which were functional in the complex everyday reality of using robustly functioning hardware and software in the classroom. The outcomes of the KidStory project are in the area of prototypes of technology which demonstrate new design ideas.

The éTui project can be seen as a hybrid of learning-driven and technology-driven approaches. The team started out with both a design area – robotic toys – and the task to explore their potential as facilitators of highly engaging experiential learning in specific contexts. They actually started from both ends. While trying to understand what children's toys should offer, i.e. what it is that would make them engaging and popular, they also used existing robotic toys to understand how young children related to them. The children had different roles: as co-designers, experts in toys and play, as explorers of robotic toys and as pupils. The result was a robotic toy designed to support playful learning through self-exploration and reflection. But in addition knowledge was gained about young children's process of engagement with robotic toys and their potential for experiential learning.

Developing effective technologies for learning requires the designers to combine approaches focusing on technology design with approaches focusing on learning. Each approach leads to different processes and outcomes and together they can, as here, generate realistic and inspiring outcomes.

$$\text{Technology} = F\,(\text{Behaviour}) \longleftrightarrow \text{Behaviour} = F\,(\text{Technology})$$

Figure 38: Complementary approaches for studying the relationship between technology and behaviour.

Concepts of Learning

The ESE community agreed to an approach to early learning which puts concepts of experiential, collaborative, autonomous, personalised and playful learning as well as creativity and self expression at its heart.

The angle on learning chosen by a project and the theoretical concepts associated with it influence how the children are approached. Concepts of learning influence both the design ideas and the way children are involved. Most projects emphasised the mutual relationship between cognitive growth and developing social relationships as originally identified by Piaget and Vygotsky. Both emphasise activity as the source for cognitive growth. While Piaget (1971) describes the development of cognitive growth as a result of interaction with the material world, Vygotsky (1978) describes higher mental functioning in the context of complex human interaction including cognitive, emotional and instinctual aspects. What makes Piaget's ideas so appealing to digital design is the direct relationship between the logic of programming and a model of cognitive growth through stages which represent the integration of increasingly complex logical operations. While analog construction toys like BRIO,LEGO bricks, Mechano etc. allow the construction of and playful insight in structures, programmable bricks or digital construction kits have the potential to play and experiment with events and 'behaviour'.

Seymour Papert's (1980) pioneering work adapted Piaget's constructivism in developing the Logo language which allows children to learn about complex phenomena by building them up from simple programming rules or 'behavioural' entities. He demonstrated the potential for self-guided and experiential learning and provided the basis for numerous educational applications of programming as a topic or means of teaching formal logic and programming algorithms. As discussed by Chioccariello *et al* in this volume, the potential of programming from learning is no longer seen only in terms of early scientific thinking but increasingly as a tool to build and control complex relationships with the material and social world. Thus it can become a tool for self-discovery in terms of potential for control, discovery and self expression (Resnick *et al*, 1996, 1998).

Among the ESE projects were several attempts to realise this potential, and the CAB, Playground and éTui projects are examples of Simour Papert's legacy. CAB is one clear example: it tries to identify changes to LEGO's Mindstorm robotic construction kit developed for ages 12 and up to allow children of 5 to 8 to experiment with programming rules. In the CAB project the team decided to involve young children from the beginning using the unsuitable LEGO Mindstorms to find out through activities in schools where the design challenges are.

Being aware of the need to contextualise the toys and provide scaffolding for their use, the Reggio Emilia team's approach to early education provided a facilitating environment for both the integration of a programmable toy into learning, and for gaining design-relevant information. By understanding themselves as facilitators of children's activities the teachers were able to gain insights into the expectations and problems children met with LEGO MindStorms. In the Playground project Piaget's and Vygotsky's work strongly affected the focus for design and the way of involving children. By giving children not only the role of players but also of makers of games, the potential of computer games for learning was explored. From the concrete contextualised activity to the abstract de-contextualised thought, the emphasis for designing a programming environment for young children was conceptually placed on the transition in thinking brought about by play. Making games allows us to proceed from understanding to making the rules. Deciding about the rules of a game means giving shape to interaction and exploring in an experimental way how rules affect the course and quality of game interactions. In workshops children took on the role of players, game makers and 'play experts'. The design team was informed by the way the children took on all three roles. Children's attempts to control a system of rules embedded in social interaction were observed and solutions were discussed with them. The dialogues between children provide verbal explication of thoughts which are valuable for the designers. Triggering dialogue was one of the design goals.

The storytelling software *Trrific Tales* developed in the NIMIS project is partly designed to give children a tool to reach higher levels in literacy development, scaffolded by word banks and speech synthesis. Vygotsky (1978) described how children at a certain knowledge or skill level when working alone can act at a higher level in interaction with a teacher i.e. in the zone of proximal development). He described the process of learning is as the transformation from verbal instructions received from another person into inner speech – self instruction. This concept can inform the design of learning software that provides adaptive scaffolding. Through observing children using prototype versions of *Trrific Tales*, interaction design aspects were identified in which children's knowledge about how to learn can be used to motivate autonomous activity. Observing children using the software included many interrelated aspects: usability, cognitive growth, motivation and aspects of self reflection. The conceptual starting point is reflected in the design of the software and in the way the children directly provided design-relevant information about all these aspects.

A third conceptual area recognised as crucial for learning in the digital domain is that of creativity and intrinsic motivation. While the former concepts allowed a more or less literal translation into computer interaction design, the latter require something like an intermediate step of translation into design principles against which a concrete design can be developed and evaluated. Conditions under which lateral thinking or creativity occurs are often referred to as being playful (Bryson, 1999; Csikszentmihalyi, 1997; Gardner, 1996; Koestler, 1964). Especially interesting in the context of early learning seems to be the recognition that '... the empathic approach needed for stimulating personal growth and development may be similar to that needed to enable creativity.' (Cooper and Brna this volume).

Most of the projects addressing these concepts focused on storytelling (KidStory, NIMIS, Today's Stories, POGO). Claims from the literature about conditions for creativity are mirrored in the technology designed when, in the context of story telling, it:

- supports shared imagination and story production (KidStory; NIMIS)
- increases the likelihood to use new combinations of familiar entities (T'rrrific Tales software in NIMIS) and
- scaffolds the construction of and navigation in complex story structures (KidPad software in KidStory)

The social and emotional needs of children were the main reasons for designing augmented environments and tangible interfaces that were at least partly away from the desktop computer. To find design solutions for emotional and imaginative aspects, design teams often decided to interact personally with the children and explicitly ask for their ideas. In the KidStory project, for example, the designs of the magic carpet and magic sofa were based on ideas from sessions with the children on possible storytelling machines. With éTui, sessions were conducted about the look and feel of the children's favourite toys and imaginative robots. These ideas profoundly influenced the design of the éTui robots. The need for more direct design questions to children possibly arises partly from the gap between concepts from social sciences and design requirements. Social sciences are not traditionally concerned with the material design of the world children interact with. There is for example little research on play which treats toys as more than a condition to be controlled in experimental settings. Only lately through applied social research on ICT in the classroom or research commissioned by the toy industry do material objects become a focus for social sciences (Crook, 1994; Goldstein, 1998; Kress *et al*, 1996; Pelligrini, 1995).

When working with children in a design process, triggering their creativity with respect to a certain design aspect can be a challenging task for a co-design session. Combining conceptual knowledge about creativity, early learning and design methodology can help establish a design methodology for working with children. The experimental integration of these disciplines could have fruitful results and provoke new questions.

As we have seen, projects differ in the directness with which they involve children in the design process, giving them the role of co-designers or just observing them in their natural roles in the classroom. How to give severely and multiply disabled children a voice in the design process is not easily resolved. The dialogue to be established needs a shared medium. The CARESS project aimed to empower expression in severe and multiply disabled children. Giving autonomy in the creation of sound through movement was one of the core aims of the project (Gardner, 1993). Children informed design decisions through their short and long term reactions to sounds they created through their body movements. The design team had to learn the meanings of behaviour and how to adjust the sound quality or sensitivity of the soundbeam technology, for example, to changing individual needs. Only through the work with a wide variety of children was it possible to design hardware and software that provided the flexibility required for efficient sound therapy. In turn, the technology also facilitated the development of a therapy process and the identification of the skills needed for performing a therapy which leaves the decisions to children who are almost never in the position to act autonomously. More than any theory, it was the children who were the main informants of the design process.

Methods for involving children

The ESE project call allowed the involvement of children in digital design processes in far more elaborate ways than is usually possible in industrial design processes (Libby *et al*, 1999). Additionally it was an opportunity and a challenge for early learning research to produce research results which could be translated into design requirements. Child-centred design methodology is a young field, in which user-centred design methodology (Carroll *et al,*1992; Cooper *et al,* 2000; Druin *et al*, 1999, 2000; Schuler *et al,* 1993; Sanders, 1999) is merged with social science research methodology. It was pioneered by the work of Allison Druin (1999) and Mike Scaife and Yvonne Rogers (1999). The concept of 'informant design' developed by Scaife *et al* (1999) proposes ways of efficient interaction with children and teachers from diverse viewpoints (for example children vs. teacher), specific to the stage in the design process (for example idea development vs. prototype testing), and the design domain (for example software vs. hardware). The aim was to maximise the variety of input while at the same time specifying it for the design issues at hand. Through several design projects an interdisciplinary body of empirical knowledge was acquired about how to establish a focused dialogue with children and teachers related to a specific design task. Druin *et al* (1999) proposed three main kinds of dialogue with children, which they called 'contextual inquiry', 'technology immersion' and 'participatory design', that give a general overview about how to shape environments and interactions which are potentially informative for digital design. ESE projects integrated this knowledge to various degrees, not least by making the authors part of their design teams.

A second obvious source of methods was the quantitative and qualitative research methodology used in the social sciences. A common feature of the projects was the tendency to use not one but several different methods to acquire design relevant knowledge. The reason for using different methods was the diversity of questions asked by a multidisciplinary design team at different stages in the process and the need to validate findings through consistency of results gained from different children and teachers as well as through different methods. Projects like éTui, KidStory and NIMIS illustrate the adaptation of a variety of methods from both design and psychology/education. (see Griffith *et al*, Cooper *et. a.*, and Stanton *et al* in this volume). Table 1 presents an overview of the relationship between intentions of a design team, methods of involvement of children and the formats of possible results feeding back into the design process. We are clearly at the beginning of working out a set of child-centered design methods which are most efficient as a complement to the scientific literature on early learning (see Siraj-Blatchford, this volume) and user-centered design methods for adults (for example Schuler *et al,* 1993).

KidsLab, a working group within the ESE initiative, focused on exploring methods of working with children in a design context. We now move on to an overview of findings.

KidsLab: Issues for a child-centered design methodology

KidsLab, an EC working group within the i³ initiative on intelligent information interfaces, provided consultancy, workshops and performance of design sessions with children to ESE projects. Our goal was to relate the world of children with the world of design so that children could have a voice in the design of products for them, and design teams could gain insights from children.

KidsLab members came from diverse professional backgrounds and represented different perspectives of product development. All share experience of working with children in product design contexts. Eva Petersson, Krister Svensson, Johnny Friberg and Lieselotte van Leeuwen from the former toy research institute NCFL at the University of Halmstad in Sweden (now CITREC Stockholm) provided expertise in the psychological and educational aspects of toys and learning tools as well as experience in designing with and for children. Mikael Fernstrom and Thomas Waldmann from the Interaction Design Center of the University of Limerick brought experience in user centred design methods, occupational psychology and also digital interface development, and Melina McKim, Walter van der Velde and Maria Romalho from former Starlab Brussel brought in competence in prototype development of digital products.

So why work with children when there is a substantial body of educational, psychological, anthropological and sociological research revealing a wealth of information relevant for design, such as that contributed by the CHAT working group? In our view, information for a design process gained from literature and interaction with children are complementary methods to be used together and applied according to the specific question that arises. Literature should raise awareness of behavioural aspects of design. Interaction with children helps to discover the consequences of those aspects in a concrete design context.

The advantage of information from research is its scientific status, which gives significant and population representative results that often cannot be found in co-design sessions. Literature can help us learn about general tendencies of behaviour. The disadvantage is that the abstract terminology of social science is only indirectly related to that of design. Interacting with children opens up the potential for a dialogue about an immediate design problem. Books don't disagree when they are misinterpreted, but children do if they are empowered by a situation. They might also guide a design team's thinking towards new solutions in unexpected ways.

Another reason to work with children specifically in the digital domain is the fact that the speed of technology development means that children relate to digital technology in rapidly changing ways and this causes rapid changes of its potential meaning for play and learning. While awareness of these changes is raised in the literature, the actual consequences for design at a certain point in time is most apparent in dialogue with the children themselves.

The reason for involving children directly in a design process is to describe a realistic possibility space for design and focus or re-focus the design team's efforts. Complementarily, the possibility space should mirror children's needs and interests in the context of activity. The earlier in a design process the dialogue starts, the greater the chance of attaining a profound effect for both sides: for the children in expressing their needs and opinions and for the design team to understand these well enough to turn them into a successful product which meets children's needs.

The involvement of children does not in itself guarantee design relevant information. Crucial to the outcome of a design session with children is how the design team's questions are translated into meaningful terms for children and how children's answers are translated back into design requirements. There are ways to successful work with children. Effective dialogue can be helped by awareness of a number of issues. During the project we were able to explore some in detail but could only recognise others. What is to follow is not an exhaustive account of factors, but rather the first findings of a journey into new territory.

Two aspects of translation

Integrating children into a product design process involves two forms of translation. First, questions from a design team have to be translated into questions to children. Then the children's answers have to be translated into design relevant terms. While Translation 1 focuses on design methods, Translation 2 is concerned with data analysis, interpretation and presentation.

1. Understanding the design question

In projects about technology for education, design teams are multidisciplinary. The tasks, perspectives and goals of various members of a design team in a product development process are often quite different but on their integration good product depends (see Scaife *et al,* 1999). The answer to a question in one domain often affects others. So awareness of the multiple goals and interests is crucial when trying to give children a voice in the design process that will be heard and reflected in design. The success of a co-design session depends heavily on the insight into the multidisciplinary aspects of a design problem by the person(s) who shapes the session. Clarifying the question helps to clarify the design problem and the design space in which appropriate solutions can be found. One effective way to understand and specify a question is to discuss expected answers with all the partners. As well as the concrete facts of the problem, certain context information is needed:

- the stage in the design process, like idea development, concept development or prototyping, for which answers are expected. The particular stage influences the space for answers, the level of concreteness of answers and the expectations about the contribution children might accordingly make between wild ideas from young creative minds to a yes or no immediately before production

- the intended user group

- the experience with products for children (a toy company vs. a computer company)

- the potential for re-design

- who is asking the question – a concept developer, a developmental psychologist, or a usability engineer – and who is affected by the answer

- the time and money available for finding answers

The object is to understand the question as well as the format in which the answers need to be delivered (for example in the form of evaluations of existing products, activity scenarios, desired functionalities, action hierarchies, in usability terms, or as information about the desired look and feel of a product).

2. Translating questions from the design team into questions for children

After the problem space is determined, the design question can be related to the experience and action space of the children. It is important to maintain compatibility between the intentions of the design team and the intentions of the children. When the question is about usability, the children's final focus should be usability, however the problem is communicated. It is generally advisable to keep the question as authentic as possible and give the children the role of experts who are able to help a design team. How a question is communicated depends on the problem, plus:

- the children's age
- group specific differences
- the context
- the children's skills

Age

To interest children a question has to:

- have a clear connection to what is important and familiar for them in their activities
- be directly related to concepts they already understand
- challenge their thinking, starting from familiar ground
- take into account the attention span of different age groups

Example:

Design question: How does one wear a wearable camera (session performed by KidsLab for the 'Today's Stories project')

Age: 6-8

Step 1 (connection to familiar actions): Started with a small discussion about the difficulty of holding and taking care of a normal photo camera while playing or doing something. When children identified with this problem we told them that people are trying to make cameras especially for children, which can be attached to clothing or the body. They said they did not know how children would like to wear them and wondered if they could help.

Step 2 (relevance of activity): If you had such a camera, what would you photograph?

Step 3 (express requirements): For photographing particular scenes, where on your body should the camera be?

But a session with the same design questions for children of 11 to 13 could have a different structure:

Age :11-13

Step 1: After telling them about the design question, give a group of three a digital photo camera and ask them to photograph a scene in break time which shows their friends how they really are.

Step 2: print out the photos and let them talk about how they made them. They will have observed that people do not behave naturally when they know they are being photographed.

Step 3: To get around this and prevent unnatural behaviour, one could wear a small camera on the body. To make taking pictures easier where, and how, should it be worn? Different scenarios in which the wearable camera would be useful can then be discussed.

Group differences affect the way questions are asked in at least two ways:

• *the focus of the question*: In asking a question about group differences it is crucial not to create answers which are self-fulfilling prophesies. There is a fine line between acknowledging group differences and confirming stereo-types. While the former creates space for different ways of relating to reality, the latter provides one-way streets of expected behaviour. For example: asking girls if they would like their model house interior to be pink or yellow is not the same as asking what colours they would choose out of a full range colour palette. A question should always allow for interpretations in group-specific ways, but should not imply them. Other differences may be more important than those implied by the grouping, a finding which could be crucial for the design process.

• *how to ask a question* so that it applies to the relevant action spaces of a range of children belonging to several sub-groups. For example, formulating a question in terms of a football game might be met with enthusiasm and knowledge by those who are into football, but others will miss both the motivation and the focus of the question. Better to allow children to choose a context relevant to them (see the example on how to wear a wearable camera).

When children work in groups, one should be aware of possible group biases which might influence the results:

Gender: For example the fact that in mixed groups boys are more likely to take the lead in computer use and control the mouse, so girls and boys might experience only one role in the collaboration. If those roles are relevant to the design question, both boys and girls should experience different roles[24]. Note that analysing answers to questions according to gender differences is only valid when the question leaves space for gender-independent answers about preferences and activities. With the wearable camera the design team was interested in gender differences. So we observed and listened to girls and boys equally. Later analysis established whether all the boys agreed about certain factors and whether the girls agreed too.

Culture: Cultural differences can refer to different backgrounds or different child-cultures. While culture in a geographical sense describes a context children are born into, child culture describes phenomena which children more or less create themselves (see for example Mitchel, 2002). Obviously the two are interrelated. It is crucial to clarify what kind of cultural differences are being considered in a design question since each has different implications for how to ask questions and in the selection of methods. When tools and toys for children in multicultural contexts are the subject of design, one has to know about the cultural differences in social interaction, preferences and experiences so one can empower children to express their needs and wishes and support inclusive design. Determining how design can support an inclusive approach to play and learning in multi-ethnic groups and how design teams can be informed by the children illustrates the need of multidisciplinary applied research.

Context of places and events: Contextualising a question happens in several ways:

- verbally by referring to a context (for example imagine being a patient in hospital)
- *in situ* by choosing a venue for a session (the hospital)
- by forming social and/or material contexts for activity (working one to one at the bedside, in a peer group outside the hospital...)

The general purpose of contextualising a question is to shape concrete requirements for action so as to focus imagination. Contexts are often used as imaginary short cuts for a known set of actions for example hospital = bed, illness, away from home...) However, children can experience contexts differently from adults and from each other. While school for one child might be mainly the place to meet friends, for another it is the place where nothing is allowed, whereas an adult visitor sees is as an environment for learning. Therefore, in a design session it is important to agree explicitly about all the interpretations of context.

Verbal reference: Simply mentioning a context (the North pole) might be enough to define this context sufficiently, for older children, but younger children need explicit information (imagine it is freezing cold, you sink in the snow up to your knees...).

The environment: Where the question asked can influence how the question is perceived. In a classroom children will understand a question as testing their abilities but they may not do so at a playground or in a museum. How inviting the venue is for the intended activity contributes to the way questions are interpreted. When a session on the classroom of the future is held in, for example, an old industrial building, imagination is triggered to think away from the 'normal' classroom into big open spaces. This is fine when the design question is concerned with the architectural potential of open-space concepts for schools. However, when the question is about the problems children perceive in their every-day environment, the boring 'normal' school building might well be the ideal context in which to focus on better solutions.

In general, the context should always communicate emotional safety and reassurance to children, since only then can imaginative thinking, exploration of the unknown or critical discussions occur.

Figure 39: children's low-tech prototypes of ways to wear a small camera together with their comments

Social context: The social settings in which design questions are asked affect what kind of space children perceive for their answers. Children meeting for the first time will feel more at ease in a group than in a one to one session with an adult. Co-operative problem solving might work better with a pair of friends than with a pair of children who don't know each other. Five to ten children is about right because the number is small enough to give individual attention and big enough to ensure diversity in opinions.

What methods to choose for a design session with children

The methods which actively and explicitly involve children in the design process can be drawn from both design and social science. The methods chosen must achieve compatibility between the intentions of the design team and the children.

With younger children especially, there has to be compatibility between the relevant design aspect and the medium of expression. The example of 'how to wear a wearable camera' shows how a series of questions can be used to focus children's attention on the relevant aspects of design. When children ultimately made their designs, they had their own scenario for use in mind. By making the camera (a wooden block of realistic size with the eye of a camera drawn on it) wearable for themselves, they faced usability problems – for example how to make the camera wearable at different points of the body. With the materials given they proposed solutions which took the actual design problems into account to a surprising degree.

The medium of expression, which can be verbal, drawings, 3D low-tech objects or a desktop computer, powerfully affects the focus children maintain. How to wear a wearable camera is clearly a 3D question, so children were focused answering the question in 3D. The appearance of the camera being of little importance, we provided them with wooden blocks representating the relevant physical characteristics of size and weight. Providing them with more interesting objects or asking them to make a camera could easily have distracted attention from the relevant design aspects. The material for their own designs was chosen according to easiness to handle and the problem of wearing the 'camera' on cloth. There was one adult per two children to help them when necessary.

Because we accidentally ran out of material, one group of children decided to draw their answers. Interestingly, their answers focused mainly on the decorative aspects of the camera and not on how to wear it. Even though they made interesting points, such as that a camera should look like the objects to be photographed (animal-like for animals and party-like for a party), the medium of expression led them astray from the original question.

Clearly the medium of expression should reflect the medium of the design aspect in question. It has been shown that low-tech prototypes are of great help (Druin *et al,*1999, Scaife *et al,* 1999). Often it is not the design as such but the concrete nature of an artefact as a shared object of communication which makes it valuable. However, systematic research into the role of media for expression which relates children's needs for expression to the designers' needs and tools of expression could improve the effectiveness of the dialogue between design teams and children.

Focusing on a problem and being creative and expressive in finding solutions requires that the medium of expression is handled with confidence by the children. When for example cutting a certain material becomes an obstacle, young children especially can easily become de-motivated. When this material is crucial for

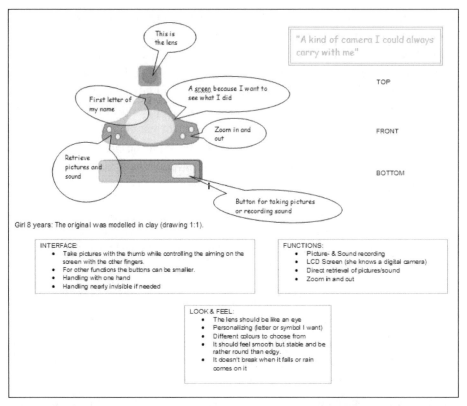

Figure 40: Graphic representation of a clay model with comments given by 8 years old girl who modelled the recording devise she would like to have at school. The session was performed for the Today's stories project.

answering the design questions, one solution is to provide adult support for fast trouble shooting. The CAB project had teachers as mediators when young children were using the LEGO Mindstorms material which exceeded their handling skills. This revealed directly relevant information for the design team, even though the material was not age appropriate.

We can support children's confidence in presenting their ideas when their own object looks good to them, i.e. is made from attractive material. But it is unwise to use material that is so attractive that it absorbs the attention of the child. The younger the children are the more important this is. A trade off has to be found between relevance of the material for the design, easiness to handle it and a modestly attractive material.

Translating answers from children into design relevant terms

Reports of sessions and discussing them with the design teams indicate the following:

- the information should be structured according to the initially agreed questions taking into account what is relevant for members of the multi-disciplinary design team

- the validity of the results should be made clear

- retain the authenticity of the information as much as possible but re-contextualise it in terms of the relevant design aspects, for example citing children's statements according to design aspects

- alongside the detailed report there should be summaries of the most important findings

- different ways of visualisation, such as tables, collages and graphs, can help make information more accessible. See Figure 40 for an example of how a clay model was used to communicate the design an 8 year old girl had made, together with her comments. The information was also structured with respect to the design aspects

- no report can replace the presence of the design team in a session. A report is selective – often unexpected aspects turn out to trigger solutions. It is fruitful when the entire design team has contact with the children they design for in the relevant contexts

Pilot research

Marcelle van Beusekom and Maaike Kneppers, supervised by Pieter-Jan Stappers together with KidsLab, conducted a pilot study in collaboration with students from the industrial design faculty of the Technical University in Delft in the Netherlands. They set out to determine the role that different methods of visualisation have for the interaction between designers and children in a design session. Over three weekly one hour sessions ten children aged 9 -11 worked on the design of a classroom where 'learning is as much fun as play'.

Session I

The first session started with a brainstorm about the different activities going on in a classroom. Each activity was written on two sticky notes. The children split into two groups and started to place the sticky notes on a 70 x 50cm base of foam board. The children cut walls from foam board and placed them on the base to create a model. We had prepared a number of model desks and chairs in the right proportions to prevent the children wasting time making obvious things. In groups of five the children discussed and rearranged the sticky notes. They tried to combine the need to work undisturbed and possibilities to move; a space for performances and workshop spaces for relaxed interaction and spaces for solitary

Figure 41a/b: Two examples of foam board walls placed by children on a model base dividing activity areas indicated by the yellow sticky notes

Figure 42a/b. Professional architectural models of the classrooms made by the industrial design students on the basis of the children's models

activities. The biggest problem was how those spaces could all co-exist. One interesting proposal was for a climbing wall dividing two parts of the room so children could climb from one part to the other instead of using the door. The children argued that climbing seemed a good activity since it can be done silently, requires the whole body and doesn't use up surface space.

Session II

A week later the children started by explaining their models to the other group. Then in four groups, each group chose one activity space on their model to develop further. They visualised their idea by cutting and glueing paper or using modelling clay, often working alone on a certain aspect using a variety of materials: paper, modelling clay and crayons. Their experimenting with shape and form increased and they tried to perfect the objects. Most of the objects were familiar game consoles, K'Nexx, furniture etc. The girls in the group spent time on details, while the boys soon became bored. The children were then offered one to one interactions with the design students in which, for example, devices for communication between the children in their futuristic classroom were sketched out.

Session III

The design students had made professional architectural and object models based on the children's architectural models and communication devices. They provided collages of colour groupings and moodboards to suggest different ways they might look and feel. They wanted the children to operate as a review panel and evaluate:

> whether the designers had correctly understood their designs
> what solutions seemed realistic
> to decide what the colours and moods should be

Main results
Shared focus of children and designers
- Session I provided the highest learning curve for both the designers and the children. In this session the questions were clear and the medium of expressing answers maintained the focus of attention. The children's thinking became increasingly insightful. The fact that they had to suggest the relevant activities themselves added to their feeling of expertise and motivated them to solve the problems they met. The size of the model was chosen to suit both group work and relatively coarse cutting work.

How to define work in progress

- Session III made the children feel very proud and that they were taken seriously. But the perfect look of the professional models led them to believe that the process was complete and that suggesting changes would be unnecessary and unfair. Talking about the models instead of making them was problematic. The idea of three different solutions for one problem (in the case of the communication device) seemed to them a waste of time, not a good basis for discussion. The same applied when children were asked to design more than one solution for a particular problem.

Imaginative leaps

- The imaginative step from the collages to the reality of a people-size classroom was clearly too great for the children to take. It did not help that the classroom they were designing would not be built at once.

The influence of medium for expression

- In Session II it was clear how the medium of expression – pieces of A3 paper, scissors and glue vs. drawings with crayons or clay models – influenced the resulting shapes of the objects, the level of detail and the experimenting with colour. However, maybe even through the choice of materials for expression, the focus of attention, or inattention, contributing towards the process of making an object instead of thinking about representations of different design solutions. In Session II particularly, gender seemed to strongly influence the nature and the details of the solutions chosen.

Implications for further research

Scientific research on certain topics would help develop child-centered design methods. The research should:

- explore and adapt the use of visualisation techniques drawn from participatory design methodology for children

- explore the relationship between objects produced by the designers and those produced by children as active participants in the iterative processes of design

- enhance the understanding of the interactive process of creating and sustaining a focus of attention in design contexts depending on age

- understand the complexity involved in choosing a medium of expression

The ESE projects offer many insights into how the involvement of children in design processes can enhance the process as well as its products. Many complex relationships between children, adults and artefacts still need to be fully understood before a toolbox of methods for child-centered design can be constructed. But no toolbox will give the most important prerequisites: curiosity, respect and empathy for children.

Acknowledgments

The KidsLab working group was funded by the European Commission i³ programme. We wish to thank all the children and teachers in different countries who took part in sessions, and also students and staff from the University of Halmstad in Sweden and the Technical University of Delft and the i³ community for their helpful discussions.

Final words

Technology education has traditionally been concerned with supporting children in the design and production of various products, and in the development of craft skills and knowledge. Too often, the popular view has been that technology lies outside of 'culture', that it is an inescapable and largely uncontrollable by-product of human enlightenment, sometimes even undesirable but nonetheless essential. From this perspective human history is seen as a linear progression in the acquisition of knowledge about the world and how it works. According to this account, as scientific knowledge is applied, new technologies have emerged and these, in turn, influence the ways in which we live. Technology is seen as shaping society rather than being shaped by it.

Thankfully, a quite different and ultimately more optimistic perspective on technology has gained ground in recent years. Technology is seen as a social product, determined by human needs and wishes. This view has been strengthened by historical and sociological studies that have shown that scientific progress has followed no simple linear pattern. That far from revealing an ever more complete reflection of reality, science has merely developed a succession of elaborate alternative paradigms or models with which explanations of observed phenomena have been made. It has become clear that technological developments often precede scientific development, and the over simplistic concepts of technology as applied science have thus been largely discredited.

One of the most significant things learned in the i³ ESE initiative is that progressive new technologies can be successfully developed when adults, children, educationalists, engineers and designers collaborate creatively. This is important because collaborative technological innovation is essentially also democratic technological innovation. It is children, their parents and their teachers who have to live with new educational technologies after they have been developed. They are usually in the best position to judge how to deal with the design trade-offs that are an inevitable part of the development process. Their value positions, expertise and lived experiences therefore need to be taken into account.

The following statements reflect the commitment of members of the i³ ESE research community to creative collaboration (Caenepeel, 2003):

> What I realised only much later was that the i³ initiative had created something like the small freetowns that we had in the Netherlands and in Scandinavia back in the seventies: a place where everything is possible and where people live in a happy state of anarchy outside the official state. The point is not that i³ was a hippie thing but rather that whatever you may think of it, i³ and i³net created this space of freedom and anarchy that I think is the soil for any really new creation. And it worked. (Job Rutgers, Senior Design Consultant at Philips Design Eindhoven, involved in POGO)

> i³ was a great adventure – it widened my horizons and explored issues of research and development which could not be touched on by projects alone. The sharing of quite different philosophies, research aims and methodologies and the interaction with society, industry and commercial exploitation has created a clearer identity for the work I do and a confidence in my relationships with partners which would have taken much longer otherwise. (Richard Millwood, Reader and Apple Distinguished Educator at Ultralab, Anglia Polytechnic University, involved in the éTui project, and a member of the i³ Coordinating Group)

> We miss it [i³]...the regular bi-annual commitment, the developing community, and especially the multiprofessional discussions around shared problems. If we ever are involved in developing a research and development programme from scratch we would use it as a model. (Ingrid Pramling Samuelson, Professor at the Department of Education, Göteborg University, coordinator of the CHAT working group)

Notes

1   'i-cubed'

2   The use of the term 'scheme' as opposed to 'schema' in this context is deliberate. As Athey (1990) has suggested, the difference between schemes and schema represents fundamental differences between operative and figurative thinking (See also Siraj-Blatchford, J. and Siraj-Blatchford, I., 2002)

3   The public reports produced by the éTui project are available at http://www.ultralab.ac.uk/projects/étui/documentation/index.htm

4   The three partner schools were CEP Robert Graves, Deià, Balears, Spain; Hollyfields School, Brentwood, England; and Birralee, Trondheim.

5   Vygotsky, L. (1982). *Sobranie sochinenii, Tom pervyi: Voprosy teorii i istorii psikhologii* [Collected works, vol.I: Problems in the theory and history of psychology]. Moscow, Izdatel'stvo Pedagogika., p. 166, cited in Cole, M. and J. V. Wertsch

6   Papert had worked with Piaget on how technology could be used to support the development of children's mathematical abilities from 1958 to 1963, and was also aware of Grey Walter's work.

7   For example, noting the fascination which children have with creating patterns from beads, Resnick and his group, created Programmable Beads, 'designed to engage children in dynamic patterns', Resnick, M., F. Martin, *et al* (1998).

8   We refer to coordination as understood in the autopoietic theory of Maturana and Varela. Conversation theory as a means of understanding learning was developed by Gordon Pask, and some of his ideas have been explored more recently in Laurillard, D. (1993)

9   Papert has placed greater stress on conversation in more recent papers. For example, in Papert, S. (1999): 'we learn better by doing ... but we learn better still if we combine our doing with talking and thinking about what we have done.'

10   See Druin, A., Ed. (1999) for a range of approaches to designing with children, and more specifically Druin, A., B. Bederson, *et al* (1999) for a discussion of participitative design

11   See also www.iua.upf.es/étui

12   The names of the participating children have been changed.

13   In terms of Beer, the plasticity of the behaviours was not perceived (plasticity is a more advanced property of behaviours).

14   The philosopher Daniel Dennett distinguishes three stances which may be used in understanding complex systems: the physical, design and intentional stances. See for example Dennett, D. C. (1981).

15 Again a stronger argument could come from Braitenberg and Grey Walter's experiments, and Beer's conclusions on the objective difficulties of tying some predictable behaviours to the neural mechanisms designed in his artificial cockroach

16 One might argue that reflecting directly on an insect's behaviour would be more appropriate. But live insects are not amenable to children's interaction (for instance, the all important body syntonic patterns). In a somewhat different context the appropriateness of robots for working with autistic children has been proposed by Dautenhahn, K. (1999).

17 We would like to acknowledge the Playground Project team and especially the work of Ross Adamson, Miki Grahame, Jakob Tholander and Sarah Nathan Lowe for their input on this text in an earlier (unpublished) form, and Lulu Healy for her help with the literature review on play.

18 The most explicit challenge to this view has been laid by Mitch Resnick and his colleagues at the Media Lab at MIT who are designing learning systems for a 'lifelong Kindergarten'.

19 Actually, we designed two separate environments, based on two platforms. See Goldstein *et al* (2001)

20 We note that the surface changes were very easy to accomplish and had a remarkable effect on the narrative of the game (see Littleton and Hoyles, 2002)

21 We can sum up our own view on this by agreeing with Stravinsky, who stresses – perhaps to an extreme – the necessity of constraints for creativity, and views 'with terror' the 'abyss of freedom' that unconstrained expression affords (Stravinsky, 1942; pp. 63-4).

22 The gender issue may well indicate a much more general phenomenon which we are unable to discuss here. See, for example, Turkle, 1984.

23 With the contribution of Edith Ackermann, e-mail: edith@media.mit.edu

24 Meeting the standards of scientific experiments in controlling for co-variables is mostly out of the scope of co-design sessions. Therefore it is very important to be aware of and communicate the limited scope of an answer from a co-design session very carefully and point to issues which might need to be answered in the realm of social sciences with well-controlled experimental designs. However, the design of a session should try to take into account major co-variables. The results will be tendencies rather than significances.

References

Abnett, A., Stanton, D., Neale, H. and O'Malley, C. (2001) The effect of multiple input devices on collaboration and gender issues, Proceedings of the *First European Conference on Computer-Supported Collaborative Learning* (Euro-CSCL 2001, pp. 29-36), March 22-24, 2001, Maastricht NL

Ackermann E. (1991) The 'Agency' Model of Transactions: Toward an Understanding of Children's Theory of Control, in Harel I. and Papert S. (eds), *Constructionism*, Ablex Publisher, Norwood, NJ

Ackermann. E. (2000) Relating to things that think: Animated toys, artificial creatures, avatars, in *I³ Magazine: The European Network for Intelligent Information Interfaces*, n. 8, July, pp. 2-5

Alborzi, H., Druin, A., Montemayor, J., Platner, M., Porteous, J., Sherman, L., Boltman, A., Taxén, G., Best, J., Hammer, J., Kruskal, A., Lal, A., Plaisant Schwenn, T., Sumida, L., Wagner, R. and Hendler, J. Designing Story Rooms: Interactive Storytelling Spaces for Children, *ACM Symposium on Designing Interactive Systems*, August 17-19 2000, New York, 95-104

Ananny M. (2001) *Telling Tales: Supporting written literacy with computational toys*, Master Thesis, The MIT Media Laboratory, Cambridge, MA

Askildsen T., Barchi P., Cagliari P., Chioccariello A., Giacopini E., Gustafsson B., Lindh J., Manca S., Rausch M., Sarti L. (2001a) *Construction kits made of Atoms and Bits: Research findings and perspectives*, CAB Del. 25, http://cab.itd.ge.cnr.it/public/papers. htm

Askildsen T., Chioccariello A., Manca S., Munch G., Rausch M., Sarti L. (2001b) *A Cybernetic Construction Kit for Young Children*, CAB Del. 22 http://cab.itd.ge.cnr.it/public/deliverables/del22.pdf

Aspy, D. (1972) *Towards a Technology for Humanising Education*, Research Press, Champaign Illinois

Athey, V. (1990) *Extending Thought in Children*, Paul Chapman, London

Barchi P., Cagliari P., Giacopini E. (2001) Encounters between children and robotics, in Askildsen T., Barchi P., Cagliari P., Chioccariello A., Giacopini E., Gustafsson B., Lindh J., Manca S., Rausch M., Sarti L. (2001) *Construction kits made of Atoms and Bits. Research findings and perspectives,* CAB Del. 25, http://cab.itd.ge.cnr.it/public/deliverables/booklet/booklet-CRE.pdf

Bayon, V., Rodden, T., Greenhalgh, C., Benford, S. (2002) Going Back to School: Putting a Pervasive Environment into the Real World, *Pervasive*, 69-83

Beaudouin-Lafon, B., Bederson, B., Conversy, S., Druin, A., Eiderbäck, B., Evans, H., Hansen, H., Harvard, Å., Hutchinson, H., Lindquist, K., Mackay, W., Plaisant, C., Roussel, N., Sundblad, Y., Westerlund, B. (2002) Co-design and new technologies with family users. Second year Deliverable (D1.2and2.2) from *InterLiving,* CID, KTH, Stockholm September 2002

Bederson, B., Hollan, J., Druin, A., Stewart, J., Rogers, D.and Proft, D (1996) Local Tools: An Alternative to Tool Palettes. ACM Symposium on User Interface Software and Technology: 169-170

Beer, R. D (1990) *Intelligence as adaptive behaviour: An experiment in computational neuroethology*. Boston, Massachusetts, Academic Press

Benford, S., Bederson, B., Akesson., K., Bayon, V., Druin, D., Hansson, P., Hourcade, J., Ingram, R., Neale, H., O'Malley, C., Simsarian, K., Stanton, D., Sundblad, Y., and Taxen, G (2000) Designing Storytelling Technologies to Encourage Collaboration Between Young Children. In Proceedings of *CHI2000*, The Hague, NL

Benjamin B. Bederson, James D. Hollan, Allison Duin, Jason Stewart, David Rogers, David Proft: Local Tools: An Alternative to Tool Palettes. ACM Symposium on User Interface Software and Technology 1996: 169-170

Berger, A (1997) Narratives in Popular Culture, Media and Everyday Life, Sage, London

Bers M. and Urrea C (2000) Technological Prayers: Parents and Children Working with Robotics and Values, in Druin A. and Hendler J. (eds) *Robots for Kids: Exploring New Technologies for Learning Experiences,* Morgan Kaufman Academic Press, San Francisco

Beyer, H. and Holtzblatt, K (1998) *Contextual Design: Defining Customer-Centered Systems*, Morgan Kaufmann Publishers, San Francisco

Billard, A., Dautenhahn, K. And Hayes, G (1998) Experiments on human-robot communication with Robota, an imitative learning and communicating doll robot, Socially Situated Intelligence Workshop, *Fifth International Conference of the Society for Adaptive Behaviour* (SAB-96) Zurich, Switzerland

Bobick, A., Intille, S., Davis, J., Baird, F., Claudio Pinhanez, Campbell, L., Ivanov, Y., Schütte, A., and Wilson, A (1999) The KidsRoom: A Perceptually-Based Interactive and Immersive Story Environment. *PRESENCE: Teleoperators and Virtual Environments*, 8(4), pp. 367-391

Bødker, S., Ehn, P., Kammersgaard, J., Kyng,M. and Sundblad, Y (1987) A Utopian Experience, Proceedings of the 1986 *Conference on Computers and Democracy*, Avebury, pp.251-278

Boltman, A., Druin, A., Bederson, B., Hourcade, JP, Fast, C., Kjellin, M., Stanton, D., O'Malley, C., Cobb, S., Sundblad, Y., Benford, S. (2002) The Nature of Children's Storytelling With and Without Technology *American Educational Research Association conference* (AERA). April 1-5th, 2002. New Orleans

Bosco, J (2003) International Keynote, *BECTa Research Conference*, London, 13th June

Braitenberg, V (1984) *Vehicles: Experiments in Synthetic Psychology*, MIT Press, Cambridge MA

Brenna, B. A (1995) The metacognitive reading strategies of five early readers. *Journal of Research in Reading,* 18(1), 53-62

Brooks R. A (1991) Intelligence without representation, *Artificial Intelligence*, vol. 47, pp. 139-159

Brooks, R. A (1991) *Intelligence Without Reason*, MIT

Brooks, R. A., C. Breazeal, *et al.* (1998) *Alternative Essences of Intelligence*, American Association for Artificial Intelligence

Bruner, J (1983) *Actual Minds, Possible Worlds*, Harvard University Press

Bruner, J., Jolly, A., and Sylva. K. Eds. (1976) *Play: its role in development and evolution*, Basic Books, New York

Bryson, J. (1999) Creativity by design: a character based approach to creative play, in Nack, F. (Ed.) *Proceedings of the AISB spring symposium on Artificial Intelligence and Creativity in Entertainment and Visual Art*, Edinburgh

Caenepeel, M. (Ed.) (2003) Nothing lasts, nothing is lost. i³ 1996-2003. *i³ Magazine, The European Network for Intelligent Information Interfaces*, Vol 13, February

Carplay, J. and van Oers, B. (1993) Models for Learning and the Problem of Classroom Discourse, *Voprosy Psichologii*, 4, pp. 20-26

Carroll, J. M. and Rosson, M. B (1992) Getting around the task-artifact cycle: How to make claims and design by scenario. *ACM Transaction and information systems,* Vol.10, 181-212

Chin, G. Jr., Rosson, M. B. and Carroll, J. M (1997) Participatory analysis: Shared development requirements from scenarios. In Pemberton, S. (Ed.) Proceedings of CHI'97: *Human Factors in Computing Systems*, pages 162-169

Claxton, G (1997) *Hare Brain Tortoise Mind*. Fourth Estate Ltd, London

Cole, M. and Wertsch, J (2002) *Beyond the Individual – Social Antimony in Discussions of Piaget and Vygotsky*, http://www.massey.ac.nz/%7Ealock/virtual/colevyg.htm

Cooper, B. and Brna, P (2000) Classroom conundrums: The use of a participant design methodology, *Educational Technology and Society*, 3(4): 85-100

Cooper, B. and Brna, P (2001) Fostering cartoon-style creativity with sensitive agent support in tomorrow's classroom. *Educational Technology and Society*, 4(2):32-40

Cooper, B., Brna, P. and Martins, A (2000) Effective affective in intelligent systems-building on evidence of empathy in teaching and learning. In Paiva, A., (ed.), *Affect in Interactions: Towards a New Generation of Computer Interfaces*, pages 21-34. Springer, Berlin

Comunei Reggio Emilia (2000a) *Approaches and suggestions for hardware and software development*, CAB Del. 12., http://cab.itd.ge.cnr.it/cab/partnersonly/deliverables/del12/del12.pdf

Comunei Reggio Emilia (2000b) *Pedagogical results 2*, CAB Del. 17. http://cab.itd.ge.cnr.it/cab/home.htm

Comunei Reggio Emilia (2001) *Final pedagogical report*, CAB Del. 23, http://cab.itd.ge.cnr.it/public/deliverables/del23.pdf

CRE (200a) *Approaches and suggestions for hardware and software development*, CAB Del. 12

CRE (2000b) *Pedagogical results 2*, CAB Del. 17

CRE (2001) *Final pedagogical report*, CAB Del.23 http://cab.itd.ge.cnr.it/public/deliverables/del23.pdf

Crook C. (1994) *Computers and the Collaborative Experience of Learning*, London, Routledge

Csikszentmihalyi, M (1997) *Creativity*, Harper Perennial, New York

Cypher, A (1993) *Watch What I do. Programming by Demonstration*, MIT Press, Cambridge MA

Damasio, A (1994) *Descartes' Error*. Macmillan, London

Dautenhahn, K (1999) *Robots as social actors: Aurora and the case of Autism*, Third Cognitive Technology Conference CT'99, San Francisco

Dennett, D. C (1981) Intentional Systems, in Haugeland, J. (Ed.) *Mind Design: Philosophy, Psychology, Artificial Intelligence*. Bradford Books, Montgomery, Vermont

Department of Education and Science (1989) *Discipline in Schools*, The Elton Report. London, HMSO

Dewey J (1910) *How we think*, Health, Boston

Dillenbourgh, P (1999) *Collaborative Learning: Cognitive and Computational Approaches*, ESF

Druin, A (1999) (Ed.) Cooperative Inquiry: Developing new technologies for children with children. Proceedings of the ACM SIGCHI 99 *Conference on Human Factors in Computing Systems*. 592-599

Druin, A. and Fast, C. (2002) The Child as Learner, Critic, Inventor, and Technology Design Partner: An Analysis of Three Years of Swedish Student Journals. *The International Journal for Technology and Design Education*, 12(3), 189-213

Druin, A. and Hendler, J (Eds.) (2000) *Robots for Kids, exploring new technologies for learning*, Morgan Kaufmann Academic Press, San Diego

Druin, A., and Perlin, K. Immersive environments: A physical approach to the computer interface. in *Companion of CHI '94* (Boston, MA, April 1994), ACM Press, 325-326

Druin, A., B. Bederson, *et al.* (1999) Children as our technology design partners, in Druin, A. (Ed.) *op cit* 51-72

Druin, A., Bederson, B., Boltman, A., Miura, A., Knotts-Callahan, D., and Platt, M (1999) Children as our technology design partners, in A. Druin (ed.) *op cit*

Druin, A., Ed. (1999) *The Design of Children's Technology.* The Morgan Kaufmann Series in Interactive Technologies. Morgan Kaufman Academic Press, San Diego

Edwards C., Gandini L., Forman G. (Eds) (1998) *The Hundred Languages of Children: The Reggio Emilia Approach – Advanced Reflections*, 2nd Edition, Ablex Publishing Co., Norwood, NY

Edwards, C. P. and Springate, K. W. (1995) Encouraging creativity in early childhood classrooms, *ERIC/EECE Digest EDO-PS-95-14*, ERIC Clearinghouse on Elementary and Early Childhood Education

Ellis P. and Laufer, D. (2000) *Meeting not Treating – Sound as a basis for communication in Music as a Human Resource: Drafts and Developments*, Verlag Dohr, Cologne

Ellis, P. (1987) *Out of Bounds; music project across the curriculum*, Oxford University Press

Ellis, P. (1994) Special Sounds for Special Needs; towards the development of a sound therapy, in Heath Lees (ed.) *Musical Connections: Tradition and Change.* ISME

Ellis, P. (1996a) *Incidental Music.* Video programme published by the Soundbeam Project

Ellis, P. (1996b) Layered Analysis: A Video-based qualitative research tool to support the development of a new approach for children with special needs, in the *Bulletin for the Council for Research in Music Education*, University of Illinois at Urbana-Champaign, USA, 130, 65-74

Ellis, P. (1997) The Music of Sound: a new approach for children with severe and profound and multiple learning difficulties, in *The British Journal of Music Education*, 14:2, 173-186

European Commission (1997) ESPRIT workprograme, Intelligent Information Interfaces (i³) *Call on Experimental School Environments, Single-Step Evaluation: Exploring New Learning Futures for Children*, September 1997. http://www.i3net.org/schools/ESE-CALL.rtf

Fast, G. and Kjellin, M. (2001) The Magic Mirror: A Longitudinal Study of Children's Storytelling. In *Third year Deliverable from KidStory*, Chapter 5.1, University of Nottingham August 2001

Ferrari M. and Ferrari F. (2001) *Building Robots With LEGO Mindstorms: The Ultimate Tool for Mindstorms Maniacs*, Syngress Media Inc., Rockland, MA

Freeman, W. J. (2001) Biographical essay on W. Grey Walter, in Nadel, L. (Ed.) *Encyclopedia of Cognitive Science*, Macmillan, Basingstoke

Frei, P., V. Su, *et al.* (2000) *Curlybot: Designing a New Class of Computational Toys.* CHI 2000, ACM Press, Los Angeles

Fujita, M., H. Kitano, and Doi, T. T (2000) Robot Entertainment, in Druin, A. and Hendler, J. (Eds.) *Robots for Kids, exploring new technologies for learning*, Morgan Kaufmann Academic Press, San Francisco

Gardner, H. (1993) *Multiple intelligences: the theory in Practice*, Basic Books, New York

Gardner, H. (1996) The creator's patterns, in Boden, M. (Ed.) *Dimensions of creativity.* MIT Press, Cambridge MA

Glinsky, A. (2000) *Ether, Music and Espionage*, University of Illinois Press

Goldstein, J. (1998) Immortal Kombat: The attractions of video games with violent themes. In J. Goldstein (Ed.), *Why We Watch: The Attractions of Violent Entertainment.* Oxford University Press, New York

Goldstein, R., Noss, R., Kalas, I and Pratt, D. (2001) Building Rules. In M. Beynon, C. L. Nehaniv and K. Dautenhahn (Eds), *Proceedings of the 4th International Conference of Cognitive Technology CT2001,* 267-281. University of Warwick, UK

Goleman, D. (1995) *Emotional Intelligence*, Bloomsbury, London,

Gorbet M., Orth M., Ishii H. (1998) Triangles: Tangible Interface for Manipulation and Exploration of Digital Information Topography, in *Conference proceedings on Human factors in computing systems (CHI '98)*, April 18-23, 1998, Los Angeles, pp. 49-56

Greenbaum, J. and Kyng, M. (1991) *Design at work: Cooperative design of computer systems*, Lawrence Erlbaum, Hillsdale, NJ

Greenfield, S. (2000) *Brain Story: Unlocking Our Inner World of Emotions, Memories, Ideas and Desires,* BBC Worldwide Limited, London

Gustafsson B. and Lindh J. (2001) *Swedish field test. Final report,* CAB Del. 24, http://cab.itd.ge.cnr.it/public/deliverables/del24.pdf

Harel I. and Papert S. (eds) (1991) *Constructionism*, Ablex Publishing, Norwood, NJ

Harel, I. (1988) Software design for learning: children's constructions of meanings for fractions and logo programming. Unpublished doctoral dissertation. MIT Laboratory, Cambridge MA

Healey, L., Pozzi, S and Hoyles C (1995) Making sense of groups, computers and mathematics, *Cognition and Instruction* 13 (4), 505-523

Heppel, S. (1999) What will your role be in 2010?, *Times Education Supplement: TES* Friday, January 15th, p22

Hesten, S. (1995) The Construction of an Archive (on Heathcote) Unpublished Ph.D. thesis, Lancaster University

Hinrichs, R (2002) A Vision for Life Long Learning: Year 2020, in US Department of Education, Conference Report: VISIONS 2020: *Transforming Education and Training Through Advanced Technologies*, September 17

Hogg, D. W., F. Martin, *et al.* (1991) Braitenberg Creatures. 2002

Holland, O. E. (1997) Grey Walter: The Pioneer of Real Artificial Life. in Langton C. (Ed.) *Proceedings of the 5th International Workshop on Artificial Life.* MIT Press, Cambridge MA, 34-44

Honey, M., McMillan Culp, K. and Carrigg, F. (1999) Perspectives on Technology and Education Research: Lessons from the Past and Present, US Department of Education, *The Secretary's Conference on Educational Technology*, Washington, D.C., July 12th and 13th

Howes, C. and Matheson, C.C. (1992) Sequences in the Development of Competent Play with Peers: social and pretend play, *Developmental Psychology*, 28, pp. 961-974

Hoyles C, Healy L. and Pozzi S (1992) Interdependence and autonomy: aspects of group-work with computers, *Learning and Instruction* 2, 239-257

Huntley, H. (1970) *The Divine Proportion: A Study in Mathematical Beauty*, Dover Publications, New York

Izard, C. (1971) *The Face of Emotion*, Appleton-Century-Crofts, New York

Kafai, Y.B. (1995) *Minds in play: Computer game design as a context for children's learning.* Lawrence Erlbaum Associates, Hillsdale New Jersey

Kahn, K. (1996) ToonTalk – An Animated Programming Environment for Children *Journal of Visual Languages and Computing* 7, 2, 197-217

Kane, S.R. (1994) Shared Meaning in Young Children's Peer Relationships: the development of practical social-cognitive know-how. Paper presented at the *24th Annual Symposium of the Jean Piaget Society*

Klawe MM and Phillips E (1995) A classroom study: Electronic games engage children as researchers *Proceedings of Computer Support for Collaborative Learning '95* (CSCL), Bloomington, Indiana

Koestler A. (1979) *Janus: A summing up*, Penguin Books, London

Koestler A. (1989) *The Act of Creation*, Penguin Books, London

Kress, G, Van Leeuwen, T. 1996. Reading images. *The Grammer of visual design*. Routledge, London

Kyriacou, C. (1986) *Effective Teaching in Schools*, Blackwell, Oxford

Larkin, S. (2000) How can we discern metacognition in year one children from interactions between students and teacher, Paper presented at *ESRC Teaching and Learning Research Programme Conference*, 9th November

Laurillard, D. (1993) *Rethinking University Teaching: a framework for the effective use of educational technology.* Routledge, London

Leontiev, A. (1981) *Problems of the Development of Mind*. Moscow University Press

Lewis, C., Freeman, N.H., Kyriadicou, C., Maridaki-kassotaki, K. and Berridge, D. (1996) Social Influences on False Belief Access: specific sibling influences or general apprenticeship? *Child Development*, 67, pp. 2930-2947

Libby, H., Risden,K. Czerwinski, M.and Alexander, K.J. 1999. The role of usability research in designing children's computer products. In: A. Druin (Ed.) *op cit*

Lieberman, J. N. (1977) *Playfulness*, Academic Press, New York

Light, P. and Butterworth, G. (Eds.) (1992) *Context and cognition: ways of learning and knowing*, Harvester Wheatsheaf, Hemel Hempstead

Light, P.H., Foot, T., Colbourn, C.J. and McClelland, I. (1987) Collaborative interactions at the microcomputer keyboard. *Educational Psychology*, 7, 13-21

Littleton, K. and Hoyles, C. (2002) 'The Gendering of Technology'. N. Yelland and A. Rubin (eds), *Ghosts in the Machine: Women's Voices in Research with Technology*, Peter Lang, New York, pp 3-32

Lompsher, J. (1999) Learning Activity and its Formation: Ascending from the Abstract to the Concrete. In M.Hedegaard and J.Lompscher, (Eds.), *Learning Activity and Development*. Aarhus University Press, Denmark

Maeda J. (2000) *Design by numbers,* The MIT Press, Cambridge, MA

Malaguzzi L. (1998) History, Ideas, and Basic Philosophy: An Interview with Lella Gandini, in Edwards C., Gandini L., Forman G. (eds) *The Hundred Languages of Children: The Reggio Emilia Approach – Advanced Reflections*, 2nd Edition, Ablex Publishing Co., Norwood, NJ

Martin F. (1995) The Art of LEGO Design, in *The Robotics Practitioner: The Journal for Robot Builders*, vol. 1, no. 2, Spring 1995

Martin F., Mikhak B., Resnick M., Silverman B., Berg R. (2000) To Mindstorms and Beyond: Evolution of a Construction Kit for Magical Machines, in Druin A. and Hendler J. (eds) *Robots for Kids: Exploring New Technologies for Learning Experiences*, Morgan Kaufman Academic Press, San Francisco

Maslow, A.H. (1970) *Motivation and Personality,* (rev. ed.) Harper and Row, New York

McNerney T. S. (1999) *Tangible Programming Bricks: An Approach to Making Programming Accessible to Everyone*, Master's thesis, MIT, Cambridge, MA

Miller, G., R. Church, *et al.* (2000) Teaching diverse learners using robotics. Robots for Kids, exploring new technologies for learning, in in Druin, A. and Hendler, J. (Eds.) *Robots for Kids, exploring new technologies for learning*, Morgan Kaufmann Academic Press, San Francisco, pp 165-191

Montemayor J., Druin A., Farber A., Simms S., Churaman W., D'Amour A. (2002) Physical programming: Designing tools for children to create physical interactive environments, in *Proceedings of the SIGCHI conference on Human factors in computing systems: Changing our world, changing ourselves (CHI 2002)*, ACM Press, pp. 299-306

Montemayor, J., A. Druin, *et al.* (2000) PETS: A Personal Electronic Teller of Stories. In Druin, A. and Hendler, J. (Eds.) *Robots for Kids, exploring new technologies for learning*, Morgan Kaufmann Academic Press, San Francisco, pp. 73-108

Nardi B. (1993) *A Small Matter of Programming: Perspectives on End User Computing*, MIT Press, Cambridge, MA

Nicolopoulou, A. and Cole, M. (1993) Generation and transmission of shared knowledge in the culture of collaborative learning: The Fifth Dimension, its play-world, and its institutional context. In Forman, E.A. Minnick, N. and Stone C.A. (Eds.) *Context for learning: sociocultural dynamics in children's development*. Oxford University Pres, New York

Noddings, N. (1986) *Caring – A Feminine Approach to Ethics and Moral Education.* University of California Press

Noss, R. and Hoyles, C. (1996) *Windows on Mathematical Meanings: Learning Cultures and Computers.* Kluwer, Dordrecht

Oerter, R. (1993) *The Psychology of Play: an activity oriented approach*, Quintessenz, Munich

Ofsted report (2001) www.ofsted.gov.uk/inspect/index.htm no. 194367

Papert (1980) *Mindstorms: Children, Computers and Powerful Ideas*, Basic Books, New York

Papert S. (1993) *The Children's Machine: Rethinking School in the Age of the Computer*, Basic Books, New York

Papert S. (2000) What's the big Idea? Toward a pedagogy of idea power, in *IBM Systems Journal,* Volume 39

Papert, S. (1998) 'Does Easy do it? Games and Learning', in *Game Developer* June p88

Papert, S. (1999) *What is Logo? And Who Needs It? Logo Philosophy and Implementation*, Logo Computer Systems, http://www.microworlds.com/company/philosophy.pdf

Papert, S. and S. Turkle (1991) Epistemological Pluralism and the Revaluation of the Concrete, in Harel I. and Papert S. (Eds.) *Constructionism*, Ablex Publishing, Norwood, NJ

Pellegrini, A.D.(Ed.) (1995) *The Future of Play Theory.* State University of New York Press

Pelligrini, A. D., Galda, L., and Flor, D. (1996) Relationships, Individual Differences and Children's Use of Literate Language. Unpublished manuscript

Perner, J., Leekam, S.R. and Wimmer, H. (1994) Three-year-olds' Difficulty with False Belief, *British Journal of Developmental Psychology*, 5, pp. 125-137

Piaget, J. (1932) *The Moral Judgment of the Child*. International Library of Psychology Philosophy and Scientific Method, Kegan Paul, Trench, London

Piaget, J. (1951) *Play, dreams and imitation in childhood*. Routledge and Kegan Paul, London

Piaget, J. (1969) *Mechanisms of Perception,* Routledge and Kegan Paul, London

Piaget, J. (1971) *Psychology and epistemology. Towards a theory of knowledge*. Viking Press, New York

Resnick, M. (1991) MultiLogo: A Study of Children and Concurrent Programming, in *Interactive Learning Environments*, vol. 1, no. 3, pp. 153-170

Resnick, M. (1993) 'Behaviour Construction Kits.' *Communications of the ACM* 36(7): 64-71

Resnick, M. (1996) Distributed Constructionism, in *Proceedings of the International Conference on the Learning Sciences*, July 1996, Evanston, USA

Resnick, M. (1998) Technologies for Lifelong Kindergarten, in *Educational Technology Research and Development*, vol. 46, n. 4

Resnick, M., A. Bruckman, and F. Martin 1996. Pianos not stereos: creating computational construction kits. *Interactions* 3(6) 40-50

Resnick, M., Martin F., Berg R., Borovoy R., Colella V., Kramer K., Silverman B. (1998) Digital Manipulatives: New Toys to Think With, in *Conference proceedings on Human factors in computing systems (CHI '98)*, April 18-23 1998, Los Angeles, pp. 281-287

Resnick M., Martin F., Sargent R., Silverman B. (1996) Programmable Bricks: Toys to think with, in *IBM Systems Journal*, vol. 35, n. 3/4

Resnick, M., Martin, F, Berg, R., Borovoy, R., Collella, V., Silverman, B. (1998) *Digital Manipulatives: New Toys to Think With. Proceedings CHI 98,* ACM Press, Los Angeles

Resnick, M., Berg, R., Eisenberg, M. (2000) Beyond Black Boxes: Bringing Transparency and Aesthetics Back to Scientific Investigation, in *Journal of the Learning Sciences*, vol. 9, no. 1, pp. 7-30

Rinaldi C. (1998) Projected Curriculum Constructed Through Documentation – Progettazione: An Interview with Lella Gandini, in Edwards C., Gandini L., Forman G. (eds) *The Hundred Languages of Children: The Reggio Emilia Approach – Advanced Reflections*, 2nd Edition, Ablex Publishing Co., Norwood, NJ

Roberts, M. and Erdos, G. (1993) Strategy selection and metacognition. *Educational Psychology*, Vol. 13, Nos 3 and 4, 259-266

Rubin A (1995) *Through the Glass Wall: Computer Games for Mathematical Empowerment* TERC, Massachusetts

Russell, B. (1992) *Education and social order*, Routledge, London

Rutter, M., Maughan, B., Mortimore, P. and Ouston, J. (1979) *Fifteen Hundred Hours*. Open Books, Somerset

Sanders, E. (1999) Postdesign and participatory culture. In: *Proceedings of Useful and Critical: The position of research in design*. University of Art and design Helsinki

Saxe, G. and Bermudez T (1992) Emergent Mathematical Environments in Children's Games. Paper presented at the *International Conference of Mathematics Education*, Montreal, Canada

Scaife, M., Rogers, Y., Aldrich, F. and Davies, M. (1997) Designing for or designing with? Informant design for interactive learning environments. In *CHI'97: Proceedings of Human*

Factors in Computing Systems, ACM, New York. pp 343-350

Scaife, M. and Rogers, Y. (1999) Kids as informants: telling us what we didn't know or confirming what we knew already, in Druin, A. (Ed.) *op cit* p27-51

Schuler, D. and Namioka, A. (1993) *Participatory design: Principles and practices,* Hillsdale, NJ: Lawrence Erlbaum

Selwyn, N. (1999) 'Resisting the Technological Imperative: Issues in Researching the 'Effectiveness' of Technology in Education' from the online journal Compute-Ed, Vol 5, http://pandora.nla.gov.au/nph-arch/2000/Z2000-Jun-5/http://computed.coe.wayne.edu/Vol5/Selvyns.html

Shakeshaft, C (1999) Measurement Issues with Instructional and Home Learning Technologies, US Department of Education, *The Secretary's Conference on Educational Technology*, Washington, D.C.

Sharkey, N. E. (1997) 'The new wave in robot learning.' *Robotics and Autonomous Systems* (22): 179-186

Siraj-Blatchford J. and Macleod-Brudenell, I. (1999) *Supporting Science, Design and Technology in the Early Years*, Open University Press, Buckingham

Siraj-Blatchford, J. and Siraj-Blatchford, I. (2002) Developmentally Appropriate Technology in Early Childhood: 'video conferencing', *Contemporary Issues in Early Childhood*, Volume 3, Number 2, 2002

Siraj-Blatchford, J. and Siraj-Blatchford, I. (2202) Discriminating between Schemes and Schema in Young Children's Emergent Learning of Science and Technology, *International Journal of Early Years Education*, Vol. 10 No.3

Siraj-Blatchford, J. and Siraj-Blatchford, I. (forthcoming 2004) *A Guide to Developing the ICT curriculum for Early Childhood Education*, Trentham Books, Stoke on Trent UK and Sterling USA

Slomskowski, C. and Dunn, J. (1996) Young Children's Understanding of Other People's Beliefs and Feelings and their Connected Communication with Friends, *Developmental Psychology,* 32, pp. 442-447

Smith, F. (1994) *Understanding reading* (5th ed.) Hillsdale, New Jersey: Lawrence Erlbaum Associates

Soundbeam website ww.soundbeam.co.uk

Stanton, D and Neale, H. (In press) Collaborative Behaviour around a computer: the effect of multiple mice on children's talk and interaction. *Journal of Computer Assisted Learning* (JCAL)

Stanton, D., Bayon, B., Abnett, C., Cobb, S and O'Malley, C (2002) The effect of tangible interfaces on children's collaborative behaviour. In *Proceedings of Human Factors in Computing Systems (CHI 2002)* ACM Press, Los Angeles

Stanton, D., Bayon, V., Neale, H., Benford, S., Cobb, S., Ingram, R., O'Malley, C., Ghali, A., Wilson, J. and Pridmore, T. (2001) *Classroom collaboration in the design of tangible interfaces for storytelling. Proceedings of CHI'2001* (pp. 482-489), Seattle, April 2001, ACM Press, Los Angeles

Statt, D.A. (1998) *The concise dictionary of psychology* (3rd ed.) London and New York, Routledge

Steffe L. P. and Wiegel H. G (1994) Cognitive play and mathematical learning in computer microworlds. *Educational Studies in Mathematics* 26 (2-3) 111-134

Stewart, J., Bederson, B., and Druin, A. (1999) Single display groupware: A model for co-present collaboration. *CHI'99* pp. 287-288, 1999

Stravinsky, I. (1942) *Poetics of Music*. Harvard University Press

Strommen, E. (1998) When the Interface is a Talking Dinosaur: Learning Across Media with ActiMates Barney. CHI'98, ACM Press, New York

Strommen, E. and K. J. Alexander (1999) Emotional Interfaces for Interactive Aardvarks: Designing Affect into Social Interfaces for Children. *CHI99,* ACM Press, New York

Suzuki H., Kato H. (1995) Interaction-Level Support for Collaborative Learning: AlgoBlock – An Open Programming Language, in *Proceedings of CSCL'95*, pp. 349-355

Sylva, Kathy, Jerome S. Bruner, and Paul Genova (1976) 'The Role of Play in the Problem Solving of Children 3-5 Years Old,' in *Play: Its Role in Development and Evolution*, ed. , SJ. Bruner, Jolly, A, and Sylva, K, 244-257. Basic Books, New York

Talizina, N.F. (1999) Psychological Mechanisms of Generalization. In M.Hedegaard and J.Lompscher, (Eds.), *Learning Activity and Development.* Aarhus University Press

Tan-Niam, C.L.S., Wood, D.J. and O'Malley, C. (1998) A Cross-cultural Perspective on Children's Theories of Mind and Social Interaction, *Early Child Development and Care,* 144, pp. 55-67

Tan-Niam, C.L.S., Wood, D.J. and O'Malley, C. (1999) 'Play initiation, reciprocity and theory of mind.' *The Australian Journal of Research in Early Childhood Education*, 6 (2), 73-83

Tan-Niam, C.L.S., Wood, D.J. and O'Malley, C. (2000) 'Play interactions and understanding other minds: a cross-cultural study.' *The Australian Journal of Research in Early Childhood Education*, 7 (1), 99-112

Taxén, G., Druin, A., Fast, C., and Kjellin, M. (2001) KidStory: a technology design partnership with children. *Behaviour and Information Technology*, 20(2), 119-125

Turkle S. and Papert S. (1992) Epistemological pluralism and the revaluation of the concrete, in *Journal of Mathematical Behaviour*, vol. 11, n. 1, pp. 3-33

Turkle S. (1995) *Life on the Screen: Identity in the Age of the Internet,* Simon and Schuster, New York

Turkle, S. (1984) *The Second Self: Computers and the Human Spirit*, Simon and Schuster, New York

Turkle, S. (2000) The Digital Future: From Rorschach to Relational Artifact, *Radcliffe Quarterly*, Winter 2000

van Oers, B (1999) Teaching Opportunities in Play, in Hedegaard, M and Lompscher, J., *Learning Activity and Development,* Aarhus University Press

Vygotsky, L. (1978) *Mind in Society: The Development of Higher Psychological Processes,* Harvard University Press

Vygotsky, L. (1982) *Sobranie sochinenii, Tom pervyi: Voprosy teorii i istorii psikhologii* (Collected works, vol.I: Problems in the theory and history of psychology) Izdatel'stvo Pedagogika, Moscow

Walter, W. G. (1950) An Imitation of Life. *Scientific American*: 42-45

Walter, W. G. (1951) A Machine that Learns. *Scientific American*: 60-63

Walter, W. G. (1963) *The Living Brain*. W. W. Norton, New York

Wood, D., J. Bruner, et al. (1976) 'The role of tutoring in problem solving.' *Journal of Child Psychology and Psychiatry* (17): 89-100

Wyeth P. and Wyeth G. (2001) Electronic Blocks: Tangible Programming Elements for Preschoolers, in *Proceedings of the Eighth IFIP TC13 Conference on Human-Computer Interaction (Interact 2001)*, Tokyo

Index